PRIDE AND SEEK

To order additional copies of *Pride and Seek*, by Seth J. Pierce,
call 1-800-765-6955.

Visit us at www.reviewandherald.com for information on other
Review and Herald® products.

An
Unexpected
Spiritual
Journey

PRIDE&SEEK

Seth J. Pierce

REVIEW AND HERALD® PUBLISHING ASSOCIATION
HAGERSTOWN, MD 21740

The author assumes full responsibility for the accuracy of all facts and quotations
as cited in this book.

Texts credited to NIV are from the *Holy Bible, New International Version*. Copyright © 1973, 1978,
1984, International Bible Society. Used by permission of Zondervan Bible Publishers.
Bible texts credited to NRSV are from the New Revised Standard Version of the Bible, copyright ©
1989 by the Division of Christian Education of the National Council of the Churches of Christ in the
U.S.A. Used by permission.

This book was
Edited by TomPaul Wheeler
Cover design by Trent Truman
Interior design by Candy Harvey
Electronic makeup by Tina Ivany
Typeset: Bembo 11/14

PRINTED IN U.S.A.

09 08 07 06 05   5 4 3 2 1

R&H Cataloging Service
Pierce, Seth James, 1980-   .
        Pride and seek: an unexpected
spiritual journey.

        1. Youth—Prayerbooks and devotions—English.   2. Religious life.
3. Seventh-day Adventists.   I. Title.

                286.732

ISBN 0-8280-1906-1

Dedication

To my mother,
for her courage and unfailing support
(even when she calls far too late at night, just to say hi).

Acknowledgments

Wow! It's finally done. There comes a point when you're writing a book that you wish you could just fling the manuscript into the abyss and never have to look at it again. But when it is all finished and in print, all the hard work was worth it. I could never have done this by myself, though.

I must first thank and praise God for His leading and miraculous signs and wonders along the way to encourage me to keep going.

Then I need to thank my beautiful wife, who is the best sounding board I know—even when she looks at me like I'm crazy when I share some of my ideas. (Love you, Sweetie!)

It is imperative that I thank Amanda Sauder, Dustin Krassin, Jeff Carlson, and my family for their input on this project. I couldn't have done it without any of you!

Of course, I must appreciate my cat, Wahpeton, whose faithful companionship has been a blessing to my life, as well as my wife's cat, Jag, whose repertoire of bizarre meows always makes me smile.

To Little Debbie snack cakes I give my undying support for squelching late night hunger pangs. I would like to express appreciation to Playstation 2 and its assorted games, which were a comfort in times of writer's block. For everyone who has ever been hit with a ball, wrecked their bike on a ramp, or just fallen down on national television, I cannot thank you enough—your pain brings my joy.

Finally, thanks to the Review and Herald® Publishing Association staff for their hard work and patience—and to Jeannette Johnson for calling at the right time to encourage me.

Thanks, everyone!

Contents

Chapter 1

Portrait of the Perfect Family

Picture Perfect

If you opened the hall closet in my mother's apartment you would find an old photo album. If you perused the pictures you would find an old photo of my father's ordination service. And if you gazed at that old print, you would note the important looking church officials encamped on the platform around my family, mustering their gravest looks. You might also note the early eighties' attire in my father's tweed sports coat, my mother's polka dot dress, and the fashionable fist-sized knots in the ties.

My father has donned his best official smile, partially cloaked in a Burt Reynolds' moustache. My mother also flashes her pearly whites, but not too much, lest it look as if she is having fun at this solemn occasion. My baby brother is propped up in my mother's arms, wide-eyed and slack-jawed, like a lobotomized codfish. He is drooling.

Then there's me: four years old, curly blond hair, rosy cheeks, and bearing a stoic smile. The smile gives the impression that I have a sense of the

11

reverence that should accompany a formal service. This smile lets you know that I have a deep appreciation for the spiritual blessing occurring. It's a smile that could only have been inspired by a compelling and proficient spanking.

See, if you only looked at this picture of my family and their employers, standing stiffer than a museum display of Neanderthals, emitting as much solemn joy and sanctimoniousness as a pastoral family could ever hope for, you might believe that we were perfect. And you'd be right—if this weren't the second attempt to capture this special memory on film.

Once you turn the page, a kindred picture greets you. The pictures are identical, with one exception: the perfect preacher's kid is sticking out his tongue. This resulted in a "delay of game"—and the aforementioned character-building experience.

My PK Personality

Preacher's kids come in two flavors: sweet and troublemaker. I was the latter. While the sweet PKs of the world possess dispositions characterized by honesty, meekness, and obedience, mine was characterized by the three Ds: deceit, disruption, and disobedience.

While sweet preacher's kids elsewhere sat quietly through entire church services without bribery, my parents tried everything from fruit roll-ups to Cheerios to coloring books. I talked too loud during Dad's sermons, performed kindergarten-level origami on tithe envelopes, and when a dear elder decided to deliver a doctoral thesis during prayer, I sought my fortune underneath the pews. My mother purchased Jane Fonda workout videos just to prepare for Sabbath morning.

My antics were not limited to the sanctuary. At school, in Sabbath school, the doctor's office, and especially at home during important visits from parishioners, a natural law put me in the path of oncoming trouble. I even stood on my head on my chair in primary class while reciting my memory verses. My grandmother likened me to Calvin from the comic strip Calvin and Hobbes.

Some people would be insulted to be compared to a socially maladjusted child, notorious for repulsing girls, making his teacher long for retirement, and nudging his parents ever closer to the edge of insanity. However, in this case, Grandma displayed a disturbing observational power.

The Calvin Comparison

The following excerpts prove my grandmother's theory.

At the ripe old age of 6 I was taken to the dentist for a cavity fill. It was

13

supposedly a routine procedure and I was told, "You won't feel a thing," "The needle is really small," and my favorite, "Novocain will help you." These were all lies from the deepest abyss of Hades.

As I lay with a mask over my face, sniffing bubble gum-scented gas (that's right, bubble gum drugs for children—you knew dentists were evil, didn't you?), they brought out the metal syringe that I was told would ease my discomfort. The sweet dental hygienist gave a knowing look, and this story would have ended quite pleasantly if he hadn't pushed the needle into my tiny red gums with the force of a jackhammer. Lightning pain lit up my 56-pound body.

"AAARRRGGGHHHHH! OOOOOOOOOWWWW! I'M BLEEDING! I'M GONNA DIE!" My mother reacted like Calvin's mom would have—she sank in her waiting room seat and pretended somebody else's offspring was crying bloody murder. She contemplated leaving and coming back later so none of the other moms in the waiting area with civilized children could identify her. But before she could, the dental hygienist opened the door and asked my mother to come and help "manage" her child.

In one series of cartoon panels, Calvin attempts an assault on Rosalyn, one of the few babysitters willing to take him on. Certainly such an act would never occur in a pastor's household—would it? Certainly an attempt to inflict bodily harm on a babysitter could not be concocted by even the orneriest preacher's kid—could it? Certainly a child of that nature should be ashamed of themselves—shouldn't they? It would, it could, I should.

14

Operation Beanbag was a breakthrough in strategic excellence. My parents and their friends had left for an evening of relaxation, leaving my brother, a friend, and me alone with a teenage girl who had the nerve to send us to bed. Our plan was beautiful in its simplicity. We would conceal ourselves underneath two beanbags we had procured from the living room while the babysitter went for a snack in the kitchen. We would then creep out of our rooms, wait behind the couch, and "jump" our babysitter while she was enthralled with her television program. In addition to camouflage we had crafted state of the art weapons using tinker toys and Legos.

But while this plan was a testament to strategic excellence, the actual execution was a testament to profound idiocy. First of all, bean bags are full of beans. Beans rustle when in motion. As we snuck out of our room the babysitter's keen sense of hearing was alerted. Secondly, while the beanbags proved excellent at concealing us, there was nothing concealing the beanbags. The babysitter was alarmed, like most people would be, when she saw two beanbags moving across the hall by themselves. Thirdly, when she yanked the beanbags from on top of us, we were not in battle positions, and our attack was stunted. I got in one good whack, but she retaliated by disengaging us of our weapons.

By this time it was too late for excuses like "I'm sorry" and "We thought you were somebody else." I had never seen a babysitter so angry, and when our parents got home we were further "debriefed" on our operation.

As I write this I am in my bedroom by a bookcase. On that bookcase is my first hardcover publication. Published in church school in second grade under the direction of Mrs. Britain, it was supposed to be a cute little project featuring the class's artistic responses to such profound life questions as "What do you like to do?" and "Who is your best friend?"

That week my dad and I had watched "Spy Week" on television, so under the heading, "What do you want to be when you grow up?" I wrote, "I want to be a spy." It seemed like a natural choice for a PK. And what made my answer so special was the illustration I used to augment my career selection.

The picture is of two stickmen. Stickman One (me) had a crude utility belt, cap, and glock 9 millimeter represented with a black crayon. He is aiming his black crayon gun at Stickman Two (presumably a bad guy) and there are little dots coming out of the gun striking Stickman Two. Stickman Two is flying through the air, back arched from the grueling agony and force of the crayon bullets, arms flailing upward, throwing his crayon gun into the air with the last of his strength. My teacher was moved and my fellow classmates were horrified.

Despite others' inability to always appreciate my behavior growing up, I think I had a spiritual gift. At the very least the situations I found myself in have provided endless sermon material to assist me in my duties as a pastor. As for the rest of my family growing up—well, see for yourself.

My Brother

My younger brother Ben had a sweet disposition and was a friendly little guy with a willing and helpful spirit. He has always been giving, supportive, and encouraging to people, even if he pretends to have a tough exterior.

Ben is an independent spirit. He seems to lack the normal sense of fear most of us possess. While my operations involved more than one person or happened so others could see, Ben ventured outside the parameters of normal mischief. The classic episode of this was when his 3-year-old self decided to go for an afternoon constitutional. To the highway median. Bravo.

Pride and Seek

My mother was the first to discover his absence. She went through the natural steps of rummaging through the house, interrogating me like it was my fault, and calling my dad at church, all the way down to circle prayer in the living room. Soon my mother received a phone call from an officer who had picked up some kid on the highway median. Ben helped the officer by telling him that every house they passed was his house.

Ben made an able accomplice. He usually did the dirty work of stealing candy, making less than Christian noises in the background when my parents had guests, and asking our parents if we could stay up late. I always played the lookout. That way, if he got caught, I could wash my hands.

My Parents

My parents converted to Adventism after they married in their late teens. My dad felt a call to ministry and pursued a degree from Union College in Nebraska, then received further training at Andrews University in Michigan. They pastored in the Midwest and enjoyed great success baptizing, speaking, and moving up the ranks of well-respected pastoral couples. And I can thank their off-the-wall humor and approach to life for most of my lunacy.

My Mother

"God could not be everywhere at once, so He created mothers" (Jewish proverb).

My mom is independent and self-motivated to the point of workaholism, a fact demonstrated not only by her work but in her love and care for her family as well. She is the apex of extroversion, never hesitating to do something loud and embarrassing in public if it would benefit her children. She is a talented singer, writer, and speaker, and accomplishes anything she sets her mind to—like directing Vacation Bible School.

Mom determined to have things flow just right. Every summer I got the Great Commission to go house to house, recruiting heathen neighbor friends to attend, so I could stand proudly on the Day of Judgment as the kid who honored his family by bringing the most visitors to church. Of course I gave my mother a hard time by not participating in the programs, and every year she pleaded with me to sing the songs so I could be an example. She was a very patient woman.

My mother is an optimist, and she did everything in her power to give Ben and me the same attitude. One method she championed when Ben or I was in a bad mood was to make up random songs and dance around the room in a way that made you want to smile—but also made you irritated because you didn't want to smile. We tried to hide our smiles while maintaining an angry stare, which made us look stupid, and thus embarrassed. Usually her nutty song and dance would win out and snap our gloomy moods.

Something else many mothers are known for is a lack of discretion regarding their offspring's personal feelings, comments, and the silly games they make up in the privacy and safety of home. Mothers seem to enjoy expounding on such personal moments, no matter how confidential. Let me share a dramatization that of course in no way resembles real life.

Many of us have had the blessing of being in a bad mood at our own childhood birthday party. We do our best to keep it under wraps, and everyone is fooled—except our mother. While everyone is looking on, waiting on us to blow our candles, our mother graciously comments, "Hurry up, dear. You've been crabby all day; blow out those candles before I do it for you."

Now everyone is looking at us. Kids are studying our expression and reflecting on our behavior that day, trying to see if indeed we are crabby. We mumble "Mooooooom!" under our breath, trying to communicate to her that we don't want everyone to know, but she is oblivious; she wants humiliation, not communication.

"Well, you are dear; you've been moping all morning; now hurry up, everyone is waiting. You can take a nap later." Shamed, we blow out the candles and talk to our friends, trying to affect some damage control.

The instance didn't matter, whether acting goofy the night before, throwing up lunch, wiping boogers on the bedroom wall, or even comments like, "Remember when you used to bathe with your brother?" My mom had an ample supply of shame that helped her create colorful dialogue for other anxious moms who visited our pastoral home.

My Father

My father completed his master's degree from Andrews University in an accelerated program with a perfect G.P.A. He is an accomplished painter and speaker. He is knowledgeable about astronomy, science, auto mechanics, and sales, and he was the only one who could ever put together my Transformers robot toys when they truly became "more than meets the eye." He is also an avid martial artist.

Growing up I enjoyed martial arts training per my own request. I never took it very far, but I always enjoyed drinking green tea on Japanese mats, learning about Asian culture, and playing with an assortment of deadly weapons which include, but are not limited to, throwing stars, sais, and katanas.

One of my favorite stories about my dad was how he blended the Gospel ministry with Old World martial arts to teach an erring brother a valuable lesson. My dad once had a parishioner who wore a slick religious mask at church, but beat his wife at home. When my dad discovered what was going on he promptly paid a pastoral visit. The man explained, "I am the head of the household. God has put me in charge, and I have the authority and strength to do it." My father gave him a new perspective by sharing a paraphrase of Proverbs 20:30, "Blows and wounds cleanse away evil, and beatings purge the inmost being."

"Look," my dad said. "I have 20 years experience in the martial arts, and I am the head of this church. Now how about we go out to the woodshed, and I knock you out cold before you hit the ground, because I have the authority and the power to do it." After meditating on that homily for five seconds, the parishioner agreed he needed guidance and counseling.

My dad's personality comes through in his surplus of jokes drier than

Death Valley. While they are funny in a family setting, in the presence of friends they're excruciating. The jokes were mostly puns or just plain strange comments. If a friend slept over and we ate scrambled eggs for breakfast, my dad would comment, "These are 'eggstra' special." If one of us didn't want to eat something, my dad would convince us by saying, "Eat it; it'll put hair on your chest." I can tell you, at age 7 body hair is the last thing you want to discuss with your dad in front of your friends.

He also had creative comments during punishments. While many parents try to heap guilt on kids for acting in poor judgment, or sit the child down to explain the difference between right and wrong, my dad went for the bizarre. Having bizarre children only added to the opportunities.

In second grade a friend and I cut out lingerie ads and other inappropriate images from magazines during a project, instead of the pictures of food groups we'd been assigned. We raced around the room waving them as a banner, shouting, "Panties! Bras!" The principal was at a loss. In a conference with my parents and me, my dad suggested a solution.

"Make the boy wear panties to school, then see if he still thinks it's funny." I promptly went back to cutting out food groups.

Home Life

As crazy as we all might seem, I loved my home life. Holidays were exceptional, with piping hot Christmas feasts on the table, trips to Grandma's house, and enough treasures under the Christmas tree to make a pirate swoon.

We always had half the church over for Easter Egg hunts and obscene quantities of candy.

In the holiday-dry months of summer, we spent time at a parishioner's lakeside cabin. In the mornings my parents led out in devotionals and prayers. Afternoons I played in the sandbox with Star Wars and G. I. Joes toys. In the evening my parents were at their best with zany games that they had invented. My father would turn on the tape recorder and tell me continued stories about him and me on all sorts of adventures, battling evil and saving the day.

Nobody's Perfect

Romans 3:23 says that "All have sinned, and come short of the glory of God." No human has lived a life without sin—no one. Many people have found bitter disappointment because they put people on pedestals and build their faith and happiness on organizations run by humans. As wonderful as people can be—as my family can be, even as churches can be—no one is perfect. And in 1989 my parents got a divorce.

Chapter 2

Identity Theft

"The most difficult thing in life is to know yourself" (Thales).

I was 8 the day my parents separated. No words can convey the emotions, confusion, and anger I experienced. If you cut off half your thumb, squeezed a lemon onto the open wound, salted it, laid it on a hot stove for a minute, then put that feeling in your chest, you would begin to sense how I felt inside.

My father picked me up from school a few days prior to leaving and tried to soften the shock by telling me about new step-siblings and the fun we could still have. It's not easy to explain the concept of divorce to an 8 year old, and he did as well as anyone could have. I didn't understand the details; I just remember feeling fearful and anxious because, at the very least, I knew the divorce would change our lives.

My mother was on edge. My brother was 4 and had no clue what was happening. I counted down the days and minutes until my family would break. The day came quickly, and only a few scattered details remain in my mind's eye.

24

My dad walked through the kitchen to the garage door and gave one last look. After he said goodbye and shut the door, a wave of emotions reached critical mass in the depths of my heart and exploded. I flopped on the couch and cried. My teary-eyed mom whispered soothing words and stroked my hair. My younger brother hugged us, only knowing that something was wrong.

The Question

Questions are a product of disappointments, tragedies, and the unexpected. Sometimes we ask why bad things happen to us or how they happened in the first place. We ask where guardian angels were during scary times and if God was on sabbatical the moment we needed Him. We ask what we will do next, what should we do next, or if we should do anything at all. We ask in our prayers, in our conversations with close friends, and in our thoughts. As my family shifted its form over the next several years a myriad of questions confronted me, all demanding impossible answers. The most prominent and important one of all was, "Who am I?"

Losing identity is one of the scariest events that can happen to a person. Especially when your identity isn't just lost, but stolen.

Dealing With Divorce

Abigail Tafford wrote, "Divorce puts you on the edge of sanity." Divorce turns thoughts and feelings inside out as people try to relate to their new life. People once full of love for each other act like baboons in court vying for kids, money, and anyone who will support their side of the story. And if you thought sibling rivalry was bad before, when there was only one person to relate to, try taking the baby of the family and making him the middle child, and another who is used to being oldest and stick him in the middle as well. Then add a new baby and a new elder sibling, and the family circle becomes a family hexagon.

Suddenly you have to divide yourself among parents who used to welcome you at any time. Some weekends are more convenient than others to be a parent, so a kid becomes uncertain of how to relate to Mom and Dad. The poor parents are forced to move and establish themselves elsewhere. New friends have to be made. A new home, a new job, and a new life must be created.

Finding identity again after so many changes became a central quest for my family. As a pastoral family, our identity was well defined. Who were we now? In the midst of adjusting to new family members, Mom returning to work, a blur of babysitters, and a great deal of insecurity, I groped around for anything that could shape my identity and help me feel the acceptance I needed. Benjamin Disraeli said, "Desperation is sometimes as powerful an inspirer as genius." I was inspired to do anything to figure out who I was supposed to be.

The Search, Part 1

The first part of my identity search came in fourth through seventh grade. I desired nothing more than to be accepted by someone, anyone. Girls seemed the obvious choice.

True, in fifth grade it's slim pickings finding a meaningful, lifelong relationship that will fulfill your every need. King Lemuel said in Proverbs 31, "A wife of virtuous character, who can find?" (NIV). The man spoke truth. Everyone my age was "going out" (a term designating boyfriend and girlfriend status, even if all you did was sit together in the cafeteria) except me.

I must have spent weeks trying to explain the "going out" concept to my parents. "I don't get it," they'd say. "You can't drive. Where would you go?" Pitiful.

Since my parents couldn't see anything wrong with "going out," I was permitted to do so. But I ran into a problem. Even though I had parental consent, wanted nothing more than to find a good woman who would accept me, and attended a school packed with girls, I suffered a major setback: Dork DNA.

Dork DNA

I don't mean that I wore the typical mismatched neon colors and wild stripes which defined early '90s clothing. It isn't that simple. You can be an external dork, which means you simply can't dress cool or purchase school supplies as nice as other kids. I was an internal dork, meaning dork DNA flowed through my very veins.

Dork DNA makes your hair grow at odd angles, forcing you to use obscene amounts of hairspray to hold it down on your head. I looked like a 12-year-old with a comb-over. Having unusual amounts of Dork DNA also put a damper on how big I got. While I was permitted to grow taller, I was not allowed to pass 100 pounds. It's like being a five-foot rhesus monkey. I was a stunning specimen.

My bad eyesight topped things off. You know what that means? Exactly: big dork glasses. Because I was active and would break anything with wire rims, I was given a pair of those timeless "America's Best" eyeglasses. They had no nose pads, no wires, just blocks of plastic. The dumb things were so humongous I had to do neck exercises just to hold my head up when I put them on. Abraham Lincoln once said, "Avoid popularity if you would have peace." That would have been helpful, reassuring wisdom for me, but I was so focused on being popular with the ladies that I went after them anyway.

Attracting the Girls

I had a lot going for me in my elementary school days. I was insecure. I looked like a dork. I walked like a dork. And because I got into some of my dad's old cologne thinking it would impress the ladies, I even smelled like a dork. Whether it was asking a girl out, sitting next to a girl with a cheesy grin, or trying to get my friends to promote my attractiveness, things always ended the same way: with failure.

Perhaps the saddest incident was when Marisa Bacon declared "I Love You Day." On this day all the girls in fifth through eighth grade would give hugs to *all* the boys. I almost had a seizure when I heard the good news. I, Seth Pierce, was going to hug a real woman that wasn't my mother. I had achieved one of my life's goals.

When Marisa approached me later that afternoon, she smiled sweetly and held her arms out to me. I stopped blinking and weakly reached out to embrace her. I quit breathing and almost swallowed my tongue. About the only thing I could do, in this clearly romantic moment, was manage to give three hearty pats on Marisa's back in acknowledgment and gratitude for the affection. I would later learn that patting a woman's back heartily during a hug, like you would a brother, does not inspire them. Marisa pulled away, crinkled up her nose, and said, "You don't give very good hugs."

My love life and search for acceptance went like this for four years. Then, in eighth grade, I made a serious deviation from my path. Before I had only lost a little interest in spiritual things. But as I entered my last year of junior high, God began to take a backseat in the car of life.

I noticed that girls had a tendency to drift toward "bad boys"—overtly suggestive guys who experimented with tobacco, gangs, and certain types of music. The girls acted disgusted at their stupidity, but they kept on dating them.

Apparently Henry Louis Mencken was right when he said, "Love is the triumph of imagination over intelligence." And even if acting "bad" to get girls is dumb, I noticed. I wanted acceptance and an identity, even if it meant sending my brain into hibernation.

My path was set. I was going to get bad.

The Search, Part 2

I was too small to be much of a gangster. My approaches to women thus far had turned them off, and being too suggestive could only go worse. As for drugs, well, there are drugs in junior academies, but I still had enough of a connection to God that I didn't want to ruin my body with narcotics. I had a hard enough time figuring women out in the first place and knew I needed all the brain cells I could get. That left music.

Heavy metal music crept into my CD library. It didn't take long before I fell in love with the driving speed, power, and aggression that characterizes hard rock. The electric guitar mesmerized me. It symbolized power and popularity. I wanted it for my own.

I campaigned for an electric guitar for Christmas. My mother saw it as a potential outlet, and bought me a white Fender Strat. My uncle lent me his amplifier.

I wanted to rock. I wanted to be a superstar. I wanted all the attention and identity that come with being the greatest guitar player alive. I was a 100-pound 13-year-old who couldn't even play "Twinkle, twinkle," but I had a dream.

Over the next three years I grew my hair out longer than most of my crushes wore theirs. I listened to more and more aggressive guitar playing. In the summer I spent six hours a day running scales, hoping for the day when I would be the best guitar player in the world and find the girl of my dreams. I don't care what people say—at some point, any guy who tries to learn the guitar isn't solely after recognition as a musician. He wants chicks.

I don't remember just when I lost my relationship with God, but I know it disappeared as soon as I started filling my heart with more earthly desires than heavenly ones. Money, women, and fame were at the constant forefront of my thoughts—and I was only 14. Any Christian influence that tried to find its way into my life via teachers, youth pastors, or grandparents was a nuisance. Church had never given me anything I could use, so I figured they wouldn't start now.

I started wearing all black, matching my darkening spiritual life. I stopped attending church. My friend Steve also started playing guitar (though his mom wouldn't let him grow out his hair or stop attending church). I now had a buddy to exhort me in my practicing—a great asset, because learning an instrument is a long process. At times I just had to stand in front of the mirror in my mom's bedroom, guitar strapped on, and pretend it was me playing, reminding myself of how cool I would look once I mastered the instrument.

New Look, New School, New Problems

In ninth grade I switched to public school, sporting long hair, black clothes, and slightly above-average guitar playing skills for my age. I was still insecure, looking for acceptance and identity from the opposite sex, and totally clueless about how to relate to non-Adventists—let alone 2,500 of them.

I fell in with the misfits. They all drifted back and forth between the jocks, the bangers, the hippies, and the preps. They knew a lot of people, but deep friendships within the group were rare.

I still had a glimmer of a connection with God, which kept me away from drugs and the parties my acquaintances attended, but it wasn't strong enough to identify me as a Christian. I didn't fit in with anyone and drifted from friend to friend, hoping that someone would notice me and give me directions to the life I was supposed to be living. I had no purpose in life as far as I could tell.

My insecurity pushed me into extreme introversion. After school I retreated home to my TV, or found relief in the imaginary world of video games, where I could be the hero, everyone sang my praises, and I always got the girl.

My first aggressive attempt at high school romance turned disastrous. April was petite and cute, with long blond hair. I was smitten the moment I laid eyes on her. We became friends through a random series of events (planned out by me) and two classes together. She was genuinely nice to me, always smiled at me, always said hello, and sometimes sat next to me and talked.

I wasn't used to so much attention, especially from a pretty girl. I began following her around like a puppy dog, showing up wherever she was, sniffing for a scrap of recognition. After awhile she wrote me a note expressing how "when friends see too much of each other it becomes annoying, and they shouldn't see each other for awhile." I was crushed.

The rest of the year I made it a point to avoid April, and girls in general. I immersed myself in the dark world of death metal, enjoying uplifting songs about suicide and the devil. Pitying myself, I spent the summer doing little apart from grueling guitar practices with Steve. I still hoped to "make it." Then, I knew, I would snub everyone who had ever hurt me. But as my sophomore year approached, I began to realize that dream wasn't quite realistic.

The Dream Fades

I'm a decent guitarist. But in a school with hundreds of wanna-be guitar gods, there are bound to be people better than you. When your identity is rooted in being the best, and you find out you're not, you feel like a chump on *Antiques Roadshow* who learns that his prize possession is worth a quarter of what he paid for it. I began to withdraw from rock, and my dream became my hobby.

My self-worth revolved around being better than everybody else. Trouble was I wasn't. I was a 16-year-old kid who was too proud to admit he needed love and help.

It's not that my parents didn't love me or my siblings didn't care. I mean love in my heart and soul, the ability to love others and *know* that you are loved. I missed that piece and didn't understand that I wouldn't find it through fame, power, or attracting enough females to make Solomon jealous. I needed to accept myself for who I was, a confused child of God who needed to reconnect to the One who could give me an identity and renew my life. But even when we can't see who we are or what we should be doing, Jesus still does everything in His power to get our attention.

God Goes Into Action

As the second semester of my sophomore year rolled into session, I was dragging my spiritual feet and losing my grip from carrying a heavy heart. God began a plan I know He has had from the beginning. He put someone in my path who proved to be a blinding shaft of light in an otherwise dismal existence.

One afternoon I stood talking to another long-haired rocker, waiting for the bell to ring after a stupefying health class lecture about bodily functions and urinary infections. A voice broke into our conversation, and a figure stepped into our personal bubbles. It was a girl, a beautiful girl. A girl who would prove to be the vessel God would use to reignite my life and restore my identity.

Chapter 3

Missionary Dating Worked for Me

"Most men and women are not looking for religion, nor do they have the time or in-clination to ask themselves questions about the meaning of life. . . . But most men and women are looking for love" (Phillip Samaan, *Christ's Way of Reaching People,* p. 59).

Missionary dating is another one of those phrases that confuses the same type of people who don't understand what "going out" means. The first time I heard it was in the charismatic church youth group. Every fourth Wednesday or so, a concerned parent came and shared the burden on his heart. We called him Dr. Love, but after awhile he turned into Dr. Guilt Trip.

Missionary dating, we learned, is dating non-Christians to "love them to the Lord." Dr. Love brought home that most Christians end up loving the world rather than converting their significant other. After all, the Bible says, "Do not be yoked together with unbelievers. For what do righteous-ness and wickedness have in common? Or what fellowship can light have with darkness?" (1 Corinthians 6:14, NIV). Lucky for me, Tiffany paid no attention to that text.

Pride and Seek

Tiffany

I don't remember what I was talking about when Tiffany joined our conversation, how she and I began swapping life stories in the last ten minutes of class, or how she even knew my name before I could ask hers. But I do know that if life were a cartoon my eyeballs would have leapt from my skull, my tongue would have rolled out like a red carpet, and I would have morphed into a howling wolf.

Tiffany had blue eyes; long, thick, beach-blond hair; and more curves than a 10th grader should be allowed. Her smile hypnotized, and every time she spoke it was a song written just for me. She dressed to kill, and yet when she touched my arm goodbye, everything in life went into full bloom.

It had been a long time since I had praised the Lord, but at the close of that school day, I felt showers of blessing pouring down, watering the parched dry ground of my heart. She was nearly perfect. Of course, I had only really talked to three women in my life, including my mother, so she could have had an arm growing out of her neck and I would still have been delighted.

Tiffany and I traded autobiographies on the phone for hours for the next week. After that, we talked for hours about nothing. Turns out, Tiffany had liked me since freshman year, and much to my surprise it was my long hair that first caught her eye. She loved rockers and guitar players. After showing off like a fool with my guitar over the phone, I had her hooked. I couldn't believe it. The dork DNA was clearing up! I had a beautiful girl who genuinely loved me for my hair and guitar playing. I knew my plan would pay off.

As good as our conversations were, I didn't really get to know Tiffany until we first went out together. One evening Tiffany placed me on hold to take another call. Waiting for her to return, I thought about how smooth and powerful I was. Suddenly my macho mind-set was blown, as Tiffany resumed the phone call in a panic.

"My mother is in the hospital!" she exclaimed. "I need to go see her, but I don't have a ride!"

Send in the Clown

I knew that Tiffany didn't live with her mom. Her mom had a severe drug problem and was involved in many other dangerous activities in downtown Minneapolis. Her dad was simply out of the picture. Tiffany had run away when she was younger and now lived with her aunt.

At only 8 or 9 Tiffany had cleaned blood from the sink and other locations from her mother's suicide attempts. Tiffany had seen and heard things that no little girl should ever have to witness. Remember, I said she was "nearly" perfect. And while this would have been a major red flag on the field for competent dating folk, I was a dating simpleton. I came to the rescue.

"I'll take you," I soothed.

Truth be told, I had owned a car for 3 months and was terrified of driving in downtown Minneapolis. Actually, I was still scared of four-lane highways. But if it meant taking this girl to see her ailing mother in a downtown hospital at an ungodly hour, Seth Pierce would be just the lunatic to do it.

Pride and Seek

My Dork DNA was being replaced by the curse of stupid.

After nearly hitting a highway divider, going the wrong way on a one way, and narrowly missing several unsuspecting pedestrians, we arrived at the medical center. By God's grace I found a place to park. While I managed a cool smile during the whole nightmarish episode, I discovered that it is in fact possible to keep on living even though your heart isn't beating.

The hospital proved an awkward situation. Tiffany and I weren't officially dating yet, and I had only known her for a week. Seeing her mom hooked up to IVs, Tiffany crying, and being in a part of town that would give the mob indigestion left me feeling a wee bit out of my element. It got worse when I was introduced. What was I supposed to do? Give mom a hug? I hadn't even hugged her daughter. Talk about my life? It seemed a little bland compared to this. I merely acknowledged Tiffany's introduction with a dumb grin and a nod.

On the way home Tiffany commented on what a great husband I'd be when my wife got pregnant, because I was so willing to go out of my way for a lady. "You would probably do anything she asked," Tiffany said. Yep, nothing contributes to an already awkward evening for a 16-year-old boy than talking about marriage and babies. I got a small hug in the car when I dropped her off, and went to bed with my thoughts buzzing around my brain.

My First Official Girlfriend

Once that "first date" was out of the way, the note passing stage began. I could hardly go a class period without writing or receiving a note. I looked through every jot and tittle she wrote for some indication of her undying love. A week passed and I couldn't stand it anymore. I construed something in one of her letters as potentially inviting a relationship, so I worked up every particle of courage I could locate and asked her out in a corresponding letter.

I handed it to her like it was a live grenade. I wanted to run and duck for cover. Thankfully that wasn't too hard, since I wouldn't cross her path for the rest of the day. I took double precautions to make sure that I wouldn't. I was going to give her a ride home after school, and any premature sighting could screw up the whole plan. She needed all the time in the world to think about my proposal.

When the bell rang announcing the day was over I felt nervous and sick. *I wonder if I could just leave her here,* I thought. *That way she'd have to call me tonight. It would be easier getting rejected over the phone than in person. Or maybe I would just see her tomorrow and she would avoid me; it would be understood that she didn't like me in a romantic sense and there would be no mess!* Too late. As I stood by my locker at the end of the day, Tiffany came bounding down the steps and saw me.

"Are you ready to go?" she asked in a normal tone of voice.

"Uh, yep." I tried to sound normal too, but I was nervous. It was at that moment she broke into a run and embraced me.

"Yes! Of course I'll go out with you!" she cried. I'd never felt such a tight embrace. I almost blacked out with the rush of joy and relief, but then she said something totally unexpected.

Pride and Seek

"I love you!"

Wow. No girl had ever said this to me besides my mom, and this was totally different. We had only known each other two weeks. Granted I was smitten with her, but this relationship had just started. I guess I didn't realize the coolness of my own hair and guitar playing. I had dreamed of this. Seth Pierce had a girlfriend. I had paid my dues in the Land of Loneliness, and now it was to be high times in the Hemisphere of Have Someone.

Embracing her, I smiled, and felt so excited I could only say one thing. "I love you too!"

Nearly Perfect

We talked excitedly over the next few days, frequenting each other's houses. It was awkward at first, trying to figure out what to do with a girlfriend now that I had one. Praise the Lord for television. TV allowed us to sit next to each other, yet gave me an excuse to look away and watch something besides her face, as I wondered whether or not I should kiss it.

It didn't take long to settle into a routine. Yet shortly after we became a couple, talking late at night on the phone, I encountered another red flag.

"I've had sex before."

I really wasn't surprised. I knew Tiffany had dated before, including a relationship that had lasted a couple years. Knowing how most teens blessed each other with affection in my school, I kinda figured she had done some stuff. So I also figured that everyone is entitled to a mistake here and there, and promptly dismissed her confession with what most people say when someone confesses something mildly disturbing:

"That's OK."

"More than once," came the reply.

This gave me cause to reflect for a split second. More than once? Did that mean two or two hundred times? I had no way of knowing. Still, I wanted to create a perfect relationship by keeping out all possible conflict and disagreement. Did I mention I had the curse of stupid?

"That's OK."

She seemed grateful to drop the subject. The red flag came and went without any trouble . . . yet.

Saved by a Girl

Although Tiffany had a fairly godless upbringing, and a past that would frighten the Crocodile Hunter, her aunt was committed to the Lord. Her aunt mostly watched church on TV at home because she ran a care home for elderly women, but she didn't let Tiffany get away with it.

Tiffany talked a lot about her church, reading the "Word," and sharing her faith. My spiritual life at that point didn't include church, reading the Bible, or sharing anything. What it did include was my bragging to Tiffany that my dad used to be an *Adventist* pastor, that I remembered a few memory verses, owned a Bible, and had moral values.

But hey, even if I didn't attend services, I was brought up in the "true church," which was far better than ongoing attendance at any Sunday-keeping facility. I figured I was the most spiritual Christian a person could ever want to meet, and I thought it was cute that Tiffany thought she was a Christian.

"Pride is the mask of one's own faults" (Jewish Proverb). I was too spiritually blind to see that I had a spiritual problem.

I suffered from a horrible programming that, unfortunately, a lot of Adventists share. We let our own light blind us to the strengths and qualities of other churches and Christians, no matter how sincere and spiritual. We write them off as simply inferior, ineffective, and ignorant of the Bible and how to spread the Gospel.

That was my attitude, even though I hadn't thought of God or church in years. As far as I was concerned, an upstanding Adventist (like myself) attending a Sunday church would be like the Prince of Wales dining at McDonalds. Yet even McDonald's can feed you if you're starving. I was about to find out too, because Tiffany gave me an ultimatum.

"My aunt says that if you are going to date me, you need to go to church," she said, wearing a concerned smile in the hallway at school.

Is she kidding? Doesn't she know who I am? I'm an Adventist! I know more about church than she could ever know. I have no need of her shallow attempt at God. I already know all I need to know. I know it all!

Obviously, my reasoning for not attending her church was sound as a pound. But soon another line of reasoning weaseled its way into my close-minded, immaculately thought-out theological arguments. This line of reasoning offered more benefits.

Seth, there are 168 hours in a week. All you have to do is sit through one hour of her "church" and you get a girlfriend the other 167 hours! You've waited forever to have a girlfriend!

And so I agreed to attend her church.

Witnessing Opportunity?

"Fine, I'll go," I said in my most impressive voice, trying to sound deeply intelligent. "So, what denomination do you attend?" I was going to wow this girl with my knowledge of Christendom as I walked her to class.

"We're non-denominational."

"Oh."

I had never heard of that before. Perhaps they were just a small developing church and hadn't decided on a denomination yet. Ha, I bet I could convert the little group with my expansive evangelistic training (cradle roll), and my knowledge of Bible prophecy (I knew there were some beasts with horns).

"So how many people attend?" I asked with a smirk.

"About 7,000," she replied, kissing me on the cheek and walking into her classroom.

That was a bigger number than I was willing to evangelize. I had no idea there were 7,000 Christians in the state of Minnesota. This was going to be harder than expected, mostly because I had no idea what to expect. I hadn't attended church in a long time, much less a "non-denominational church."

What do 7,000 people do in a service? God was going to blow me away.

The Man Knows His Sheep

"I am the good shepherd, and know my sheep, and am known of mine" (John 10:14).

In my early teenage years I had zero desire to go back to Adventism. God knew that, so God worked outside the system. God is not bound by church manuals, protocols, agendas, systems, or even natural law. God is bound by love and His Word—not because they are more powerful than Himself, but because they are the very essence of who God is. The Bible says, *"God is love"* (1 John 4:8), and *"The Lord is . . . not willing that any should perish, but that all should come to repentance"* (2 Peter 3:9).

Because He loves us and doesn't want us to be lost, God will go out of His way and use unorthodox methods to get our attention. Remember this when you see people drifting away from faith. When your friend leaves the church, remember that God doesn't leave or forsake people. When you feel like you are fathoms beneath a sea of sin, and you can hardly recall what it's like to breathe the sweet air of God's presence, remember that if God went to the grave for you, He is certainly capable of going where you are now.

44

Chapter 4

Welcome to the Big Show

"What is worship? Worship is to feel in your heart and express in some appropriate manner a humbling but delightful sense of admiring awe and astonished wonder and overpowering love in the presence of that most ancient Mystery, that Majesty which philosophers call the First Cause, but which we call Our Father Which Art in Heaven" (A. W. Tozer).

"Worship is experiential" (*Seventh-day Adventist Minister's Manual,* p. 146).

Shock: a sudden or violent mental or emotional disturbance (Webster's Dictionary).

For reasons unbeknownst to me, Adventists love the 1970s. Whether it's the bushy-haired person on the cover of the lobby literature, or the blazing red—er, orange, um, reddish orange—carpet and pews that set our sanctuaries aglow, the seventies have always been a dominant theme of churches I know. I imagined all churches that way. Attending Joyful Grace Community Church felt like waking up after 25 years in a cryogenic freeze.

Where Are We?

Driving toward the facility for the Wednesday evening service, I was struck by the fact that the church wasn't in a church. The building had no steeple, no visible cross, or even a pointed roof. Appalling. I knew for a fact that only idiots would put a church in such a location, and that no one can truly worship the Lord without at least having a pointed roof.

I thought about sharing my architectural insights with Tiffany, but something disrupted my thoughts. We were pulling into a parking lot the size of an aircraft carrier. It looked like an auto auction. People wearing reflective orange vests waved glow sticks. I panicked and almost hit one of out self-preservation, but Tiffany informed me they were just attendants.

"Just follow them," she said sweetly. "They're the parking lot ministry."

Were they mad? A ministry dedicated to the parking lot?

"I don't believe they have attendants here," I mumbled.

"Yeah, doesn't your church?"

"No, we know how to drive and park our own cars."

Intimidation

After parking the car (with the help of an attendant), I needed just a moment to stand and stare down the building for a few moments. In my mind, it was my Adventist heritage, beliefs, and upbringing versus The Living Word Christian Center. *How did I get talked into this?* I wondered. I decided to set my heart against anything this place had to offer. I had been doing fine with

God up until now, and I didn't need some church in a square building telling me what to do. For all I knew, they worshipped the devil at Sunday churches. *Yeah, that's right,* I thought to myself. *Bunch of wannabes that don't even know they serve the deceiver.* I stood there wanting just one more minute to size up this den of evil before I graced it with the light of my presence, but my girlfriend was impatient and dragged me forward.

"Come on!" Tiffany grabbed my hand, pulling me like a piece of taffy. I would have given anything to wait in the car. Tiffany gave me a look, and I knew no argument would do any good. I was going to church whether I liked it or not. And so I took the first steps toward a place that in three years, I would have no desire to leave.

The Sanctuary

We entered the lobby of the church. The carpet was an inviting crème color. A small bookstore stood to our left. The greeters wore pleasant smiles. Streams of people flowed into two huge sets of double doors leading to the main sanctuary. I relaxed a little, and Tiffany motioned for me to follow her down a hallway on our right.

"This is the main church," she informed me. "Tonight, we're going to The Rock."

"Did you say we're going to rock?"

"The Rock is the youth church, next to the main sanctuary. I just wanted to show you what the main lobby/sanctuary looked like. This is where everyone attends church Sunday morning."

I just had to take a peek through the white double doors into the sanctuary. As I did so, my mind's nice little picture of a typical sanctuary tumbled to the floor.

Someone had carpeted and placed seats in the Grand Canyon. The auditorium-style sanctuary was a brilliant array of lights, cavernous space, thousands of chairs, and a beautiful platform that could accommodate any Broadway production. As I crept a few inches through the door, I half expected to hear the chorus music movies play as a shaft of light falls on the hero. Tiffany had to tug at me to step away from the doors so we could get to The Rock before service started.

The Rock

The Rock was altogether different yet again. If the main sanctuary was modeled after a palace, The Rock was modeled after a night club. It featured a café, loud contemporary Christian music videos playing on large screens, 30 free-play video games, two pool tables, and a full-sized basketball court. It was everything the traditionalist adults I knew would detest. It was marvelous.

An unusually large man greeted us. Paul was a bouncer of sorts, there to make sure kids didn't loiter or get into trouble. All the kids knew him, and I discovered later that he was like another dad to many of the youth. He gave Tiffany a huge hug, then inquired as to who I was. After eyeballing his expansive girth I decided politeness was the best policy at the moment. At my size, I wouldn't even be a light snack for this guy. He smiled back at me, shook my hand, and led me to the check-in counter.

They wanted me to "sign-in." I wondered if this was some kind of release form stating that they wouldn't be held responsible if I got hurt in one of their pagan ceremonies. The young girl at the desk assured me that the form was merely a way to check attendance and keep track of regulars and visitors. Once signed in, I was handed a packet with a tape from the pastor, some reading material, and a coupon for their café.

Next I went through the awkward process of meeting Tiffany's other Christian friends. In my experience, people I've dated are always more excited about me than their friends are. Tiffany bubbled about my guitar playing and my upbringing as an Adventist. I thought she would pull a muscle from smiling so hard. Her friends were polite and friendly enough, but unsure of what to think of me. I was dressed in one of my all black ensembles: dirty sneakers, Megadeth t-shirt, and jeans that looked like they had been in a bar fight. I wore my hair down in my face for an air of mystery. I stood out against their clean-cut, preppy wardrobes.

The free-play video games gave me a bit of relief from the awkwardness of new people. It's a teenage boy's dream to find 30 arcade machines that don't require a monetary diet to keep them running. In retrospect, this idea was brilliant in that it gave something for an uneasy visitor to do without looking confused. My defenses cooled a bit. I also enjoyed the pool tables with a couple other new and intimidated kids dressed like me. Tiffany was by my side the whole time, pleased I was enjoying myself at least a little bit.

After 20 minutes the power in the games and the café went out, along with all the lights. Paul hollered from the door, "It's service time! Everybody into the sanctuary!"

Clever fools! They almost had me tricked. Those video games were just an attempt to lower my defenses and hinder my spiritual discernment. As if I had any.

The Rockatorium

They herded us through glass doors at the back of the lobby/rec area into a semi-finished warehouse room. *This is the sanctuary?* It looked like an academy gym. Painted in grey tones, it had more lighting than the lobby/rec area. Stage lighting fixtures clung to the steel beams on the ceiling. They called it the Rockatorium.

On the north and west sides were huge sets of bleachers. In between the bleachers a couple goof-ball looking people ran the equipment in the sound-booth. They were laughing and having way too much fun to be in church.

"If this service goes longer than an hour, I'll need a sling for my rear," I said, sitting down beside Tiffany on unpadded bleachers. Tiffany ignored my comment, and together we looked at the largest spectacle of The Rock—the stage.

It was 20-feet long, black carpeted, with a digital drum-set in one corner. The background was neon-colored brick that glowed under the blacklights, with spray-painted designs making the backdrop look like an alleyway. A working lamppost and two massive video screens flanked the stage 15 feet above the floor.

If I had been in my right mind at the time I would have readily admitted that this was the greatest setup I had ever seen. But I was being a party pooper, and when Tiffany pointed things out to me, I played them off like they weren't very impressive.

My First Charismatic Church Service

The floodlights dimmed, the spotlights came on, and the service started with the drama team. An announcer from the sound booth boomed, "Ladies and gentlemen, Streetlight Drama!"

"Named after the lamppost—nice," I whispered.

After the applause diminished and the skit ended, even I had to admit they were good. Their skit was funny and a grin escaped me once or twice. Tiffany noticed and smiled, and then I noticed she was sitting almost a foot away from me. I asked why she was sitting so far away, and then she explained to me the dumbest thing I had ever heard of.

"I can't sit closer; they have a six-inch rule."

"A what?" I barked, startling some worshipers.

"A six-inch rule. Guys and girls have to sit six inches apart so they won't be distracted by each other."

Of all the fruity ideas! There went my plan B if the service got dry. What was I supposed to do now? Tiffany was firm on this point, despite several others in The Rockatorium having a clear disregard for it. This meant I would actually have to listen and participate. As I pouted, High Praize took the stage.

High Praize was a group of youth musicians who would give you blank stares if you requested "Kum Ba Yah." The worship leader was a young adult in his late twenties, and everybody else looked my age. The drummer had dark hair and a beard, and suddenly he started up tight and quick. Following suit, the girl on the keyboard laid down a melody and without prompting everybody in the Rockatorium leapt to their feet, clapping with the rhythm. Not wanting to look like an oddball, I joined the happy throng, standing and even clapping a little. But then they did something frightening.

Hand Raising

"Everyone raise your hands in praise to the Lord," the worship leader called. Hands everywhere rocketed upward, making the Rockatorium look like it was in the middle of a hold up. It wasn't a quick act either. People left their hands raised for one, two, even three songs! Tiffany was doing it like it was the most natural thing in the world. I tried to join in, but couldn't get my hands past handshaking height. Having never truly worshipped before—with energy, concentration, contrition, and surrender—I found it a draining experience.

Eventually the praise and worship music grew slower and gently faded into simple melodies and occasional choruses. Teenagers knelt in prayer. Some were crying. Others sang from their hearts. The spotlights shifted to blues, purples, and other cooler tones. I felt sleepy, partly because the music was so beautiful and relaxing, and partly because I hadn't been conditioned to standing in a worship service longer than one hymn.

The Aftermath of Worship

When we finally sat down for the announcements, I felt dazed. I wasn't sure what to think about what I had just witnessed. The drama was professional. The music was dynamic, powerful, and worshipful. The lights and stage setting worked with the presentations. People participated in the song service. They felt something. It scared me. Most of the people I knew didn't respond during church, save for the occasional "Good morning" mumbled back at the pastor. *I wonder what moves them so much . . . Bah, it doesn't matter; if it was truly something worthwhile I would have felt it by now.* I changed my expression from wonderment back to gruff.

Granted, the music was good, along with the drama, but they could have gotten lucky. *They probably do the same skit every week. And raising hands? Please, how crazy can you get? If God wanted us to raise our hands in worship services we'd be doing it in the Adventist church.* I concluded that these people wouldn't know truth if it leapt out of Revelation 14 and blew a trumpet in their ears. I determined to resist The Rock's ministry. Then God played a trump card. Steve Munds, the greatest youth pastor to walk the fair land of Minnesota, took the stage.

Pastor Steve

He bounded up the platform steps like Tigger from Winnie the Pooh. His custom pulpit matched the street theme. He was in his forties but dressed like he was 18. He sported a goatee, Elvis impressions, and more energy then a 6-year-old on sugar pills. He wore a smile the size of Texas and bounced around as he preached. "I'm preaching myself happy!" he'd exclaim. "I'm preaching better than you're responding."

Instead of "Amens" he would sometimes simply start snapping his fingers, sparking teens to join in. On one occasion Pastor Munds made his way over to a gothic-dressed guy who looked beyond bored. Without breaking his sermon or missing a beat, Pastor Munds sat on his lap and preached right to him. The kid couldn't help but grin, and the rest of us paid attention so it wouldn't happen to us.

But what made this spectacle of a preacher powerful and captivating was that his words were just as effective as his stage presence. While he danced around, smiling, making loony faces to compliment his fantastic stories, he would open his Bible and preach the Word at its core. His sermon that evening included no dry exegetical analysis of the text, no worn out illustrations, and no fancy words. He simply reached into the Word, grabbed its truth, shoved it into your life, and challenged you to keep it there. Incredible. I had never connected with a speaker like this.

Tiffany leaned over, ecstatic. "We usually have a guest speaker on Wednesday nights," she whispered. "Pastor Steve preaching tonight must be a divine appointment!"

I nodded, thinking, *What on earth is a divine appointment?* Pastor Munds finished with an altar call. Tiffany and I stayed in the bleachers.

What's That Noise?

Then I heard something that sent electric ice up my spine. It was another language, or, at least it sounded like another language. Tongues! Several weeks ago Tiffany had mentioned that people here "prayed in the spirit," but I didn't pay it much attention. I dismissed it somehow in my mind and pretended Tiffany was talking about something else. But as I sat in that sanctuary, with those sounds coming from the people's mouths, my skin turned as cold as the steel bleachers I sat on.

The Adventists I knew regarded tongue talkers with mortal terror, claiming that they are all possessed by the devil and things of that nature. I was pre-programmed to go on the defensive. I had heard people talk about feeling an evil presence when they heard it, so I knew what I should feel. But I couldn't just run out of the service screaming like a nut—Tiffany wouldn't understand. *I need some way to rationalize this!*

Then it struck me. There were a few Hispanic kids attending. I found my escape from the terror. I simply put on a smile, relaxed, and pretended we had all just entered the Spanish portion of this service.

Personal Relationship?

I knew I had to talk to the pastor about his preaching. It had struck a chord with me that I didn't know I had. It was well presented and dynamic, and unlike the sermons my previous youth pastors gave, insanely practical. I wanted to express my gratitude for his ministry, for the new feeling I had felt, for hearing the Word of God preached with spiritual power for the first time. But all I could say as I shook his hand was, "Good message."

He graciously accepted the compliment and expressed his joy in my attendance. I told him I was an Adventist, expecting a rebuttal or a look of awe. I figured he would either be impressed by my spiritual aura, or repulsed because his faith was so inadequate to mine. He merely affirmed my beliefs and said he was glad I had a "personal relationship" with Jesus Christ.

We left quickly after that, Tiffany squealing and giggling, peppering me with questions about her church. I half-heartedly answered her. The pastor's comment about a "personal relationship with Jesus" had shaken me. What did he mean? Sure I had one—didn't I?

I decided that maybe I'd keep going to church with Tiffany for awhile and keep troubleshooting The Rock for heresy. I also wanted to think about this personal relationship business some more.

Knowing the Truth Doesn't Mean Knowing It All

"But God hath chosen the foolish things of the world to confound the wise" (1 Corinthians 1:27).

In my spiritual pride I believed I was wise. I had studied the Bible and been baptized in the remnant church, and thought the idea of a Sunday-keeping girl contributing to my spiritual life was absurd.

Adventists sometimes skip over the power behind the Message, namely, a personal relationship with Jesus Christ. I don't know how many Adventists have looked at me weird when I asked the simple question, "Do you know Jesus?" I believe that should be the first question asked on the baptismal vow. Everything else is irrelevant unless it applies to your relationship with Jesus. Gold stars for memory verses are nice, but they are no substitute for stars in a golden crown, given by Christ Himself. Take time from distinguishing yourself as a part of the "chosen," and ask yourself if you have chosen Jesus Christ as your *personal* Lord and Savior. You might be surprised to see how much of your spiritual life is governed by pride and the sin of self love (because this is what I've always been taught), as opposed to humility and love for God and your neighbor. Ask yourself the hard question, "Do I *know* Jesus?"

Chapter 5

Trouble in the Mission Field

"Can two walk together, except they be agreed?" (Amos 3:3).

I thought I could do it. I thought it was all about me. I thought I could steal God's worship just a little bit and He wouldn't notice. I thought I could go along for the ride without making a commitment. I thought I could join High Praize as a lead guitarist, impress everyone when I played, have Tiffany stay with me because I looked spiritual, and never have to change my life or lose my spiritual pride. I thought there was nothing wrong serving my girl-friend's needs under a disguise of serving God. After a month of attending The Rock, I thought this was the perfect plan.

Fooling Myself
"Do not, like the hypocritical Pharisees, do things to make you appear devotional and righteous in the eyes of others" (*Testimonies*, vol. 1, p. 87).

I had everybody fooled—especially myself. I kept my bitter prideful spirit while managing to pull off looking like a regular upstanding member of The Rock, playing with the praise and worship team. Even the Pope would have believed that I was a sincere Christian, simply wanting to serve the Lord with my gift. I was about to learn that ministry is not self-serving, and that no one can serve two masters (Matthew 6:24). When you accommodate both the world and Christianity in your heart, there is going to be a rumble. The truth must come out; you can't fake being a Christian forever.

Woman Worship

My relationship with Tiffany had reached the two-and-a-half month mark, and things couldn't seem better. She was my all in all. I trusted her more than anyone. She owned my heart. I stopped hanging around my other friends so I could spend all my time with Tiffany. I was ministering at The Rock for her. I had truly forsaken all and taken up my burden so I could follow wherever she went. I no longer tried to find my self-worth in rock and roll, and my depression had slipped away. I had found salvation.

God had removed me from my lonely life and into one with more love and acceptance, and one that would bring me in contact with church. Yet God's plan wouldn't end here. I still wasn't serving Him from my heart, and I still hadn't relinquished the spiritual pride I didn't know I had. I hadn't yet learned to surrender to Him.

God had known I wouldn't accept Him through literature, an evangelistic series, or even through another Adventist. Instead He carefully wove a plan, custom-built to catch me. Knowing my desire for a girlfriend and my know-it-all attitude, God worked through Tiffany to bring me back in contact with church.

"God works for the good of those who love him" (Romans 8:28, NIV). As cracks and fault lines appeared in my relationship with Tiffany, God began to repair the rubble that was my relationship with Him. He had removed my life from its dependence on musical aspirations and hopeless secularism. Now He would remove my life from Tiffany's, placing it in His hands once and for all.

Worst Case Scenario

The biggest red flag, and start of trouble, in my relationship with Tiffany came as we chatted one night on the phone. She sounded shaken and nervous. I asked her what was wrong, prepared to be the manly comforter who would come to the rescue. What she said deflated my puffed-up chest.

"What is the worst thing that could happen in our relationship?" she asked.

I hate questions like that. The question sucked the breath right out of me, and my mind began a file search for the worst case scenario. I felt my stomach sink lower and lower as my mind crept closer to the inevitable answer.

"You slept with an ex-boyfriend," I said frankly. I couldn't believe it had come out like that. There was a long pause.

"Yes . . ."

I don't remember the specific things I said to Tiffany after that, but I do know it was in the spirit of "We can work this out." I fought to keep the relationship. No matter the cost, I didn't want another broken relationship in my life. Tiffany was ashamed and didn't seem interested in salvaging our love. As my heart broke and my mouth talked faster than ever, she said goodbye and hung up.

I sat blankly on the couch and let my mind whirl around and around about every date, every kiss, and every promise Tiffany and I had shared over the past couple months. I knew she had slept around in the past. I knew she still had calls from her bozo ex-boyfriends. What I didn't know was how much of my self-worth and identity I had poured into this girl.

I couldn't go back to being lonely. I mustered up my courage, wiped the tears away, and did the most profound and meaningful act a high school boy can do for his girl when it doesn't look like she wants to be with him anymore. I wrote her a note.

God Removes My Idol

The note mended our relationship like a band-aid on a severed head. While she accepted the note and reinstated our relationship, the damage was done. Her dishonesty set off a chain reaction of distrust. Emotional stress and mind games became the norm over the next three weeks.

"Seth . . . will you drive me to the teen clinic?"

I sat in the waiting room while they examined my 16-year-old girlfriend to see if she was pregnant or worse. I glanced at pamphlets about topics I'd giggled about in elementary school. Now they didn't seem so funny. As my mind whittled away possible scenarios for the next several years of my life, depending on Tiffany's prognosis, she came out of examination for a five-minute break.

"They say I should go to the hospital to have an ultrasound." Then she walked off without another word. How beautifully vague.

Is she pregnant? What is going on? Rage swelled within me, but I cooled myself down and stuffed my feelings away, not wanting to rock our already leaky love boat. *I have to be strong for her.* Not expressing my feelings was a good thing—wasn't it? I was going to put her first in everything and become the hero I always wanted to be. I continued to stew about my options for the future if she was indeed pregnant.

Thankfully, she wasn't. She informed me as we left the clinic, along with the line, "Promise you'll never leave me?" Her hand clung to mine as I reassured her, "I'm going to marry you."

Despite such vows, our relationship continued its freefall. From my music to my shoes, Tiffany suddenly found everything about me unattractive and unacceptable. For the first time I argued back, no longer afraid of what she would say. Tiffany began hanging out with my best friend Steve instead of me.

The End of Romance

At that point my life had only two focuses: Attending The Rock, and attending to my rocky relationship. I had quit participating in High Praize, because I didn't feel like playing when my girl wasn't watching. The truth was,

I couldn't keep up with them. They spent practices in long prayer sessions and discussed spiritual topics. I just wanted to play guitar for my adoring fans. You can't be in a spirit-led ministry if you don't have an active spirit, and I became agitated with everyone.

As for Tiffany, she attended church with me but, caught up with some of the other youth at The Rock, she didn't pay me much attention. I was no longer spiritual enough for her. My religious mask had worn through, and she could see that I wasn't all I made myself out to be. I also began to see more and more sides of Tiffany that revealed she wasn't all she made herself out to be either. During the week she started hanging out with some of her old friends who weren't Christians and participating in some of their "fun." Then she attended church and acted like she was a spiritual superstar.

Sort of like I was doing.

We were both searching for someone to give the kind of love only God can give. And no matter how many spiritual friends, good relationships, or caring parents a person has, there is only one way to God. I couldn't stay with Tiffany, depending on her for everything, and still grow closer to God.

"Seth? You know that we have to break up, right? It only makes sense. I need to grow as a Christian, and you just haven't made that commitment." Click. Dial tone.

Break Ups and God's Leading

I had to clean an outhouse at campmeeting once, and it stunk so bad

63

they could have bottled the scent and called it *Purgatory*. Breaking up was worse, much worse.

After sticking through all her mess I got the brush off like I was some leech draining the life blood out of her? If anything, I was the one holding her fragile Christian experience in place and keeping her going in life! At least that is what she'd told me so many times. I wanted to call her back and call her every name I could think of, which would include, but not be limited to, "Irrational! Hypocrite!" and . . . "Please take me back?"

Love and hate swirled in my heart and fought their way down to my stomach. I had to go sit on the couch and feel sorry for myself.

Jesus Knew What Would Work

"I am the good shepherd; I know my sheep and my sheep know me" (John 10:14, NIV).

Sulking on the sofa, I began searching for what to do next. I was asking deep questions and thinking even deeper thoughts.

It's not easy reaching stubborn lukewarm teenagers who believe they know everything because they were "brought up in the church." Fortunately, Jesus knows us so well that He can even use our sinful desires to bring us to His throne. He did it for me. I wanted women and fame through guitar playing. I thought that would fill my soul. Jesus used a girl and an opportunity to play guitar to bring me to a place that made me question my spiritual life. A place that planted seeds in me, even though I didn't think I was listening.

I had nothing left. Rock and roll hadn't mattered for weeks now. Tiffany and church were all I had made time for—especially Tiffany. Now she was gone. I couldn't go hang out with my public school friends—I hadn't spent time with them at all since I started dating. I began thinking about what I'd done before I dated Tiffany, and didn't want to go back. Church wasn't a priority to my family at the time, and even if it was, the local Adventist church at that time was boring and irrelevant to a kid who feels like he's drifting through life.

I spotted something on the arm of the couch. For the first time I felt deeply impressed to open the Bible and read. It was a strange sense in my spirit. I had another option. An option that I had been so close to for the last three months and never realized it was there.

God Speaks Through His Word

Turning to the book of Job, I found the story of my life. The ancient patriarch lost it all, from family to wealth to health. Friends couldn't help him, loved ones abandoned him, and his supportive wife suggested he "curse God and die." *That's how I feel.* God had my attention, and then He went for my heart.

"And the Lord restored the fortunes of Job when he had prayed for his friends; and the Lord gave Job twice as much as he had before" (Job 42:10, NRSV). Job regained everything when he prayed to God. I couldn't remember the last time I had really prayed with my whole heart. I contemplated my spiritual life. *Did I even have a personal relationship with Jesus before?* The answer was

swift and forceful. All I had ever possessed was the title of a denomination, and the Bible is clear that only one name saves us.

What I Needed

I wanted a pity party, but the Holy Spirit crashed it. I wanted to camp on the couch and ruminate about how unfair love was, but the Holy Spirit wouldn't leave me alone. I wanted some time to think, but the Holy Spirit impressed my mind. I wanted to wallow in my misery—the Holy Spirit helped me tie my shoes, put on my coat, and get in my car. I needed just one second to doubt, but the Holy Spirit filled me with faith and removed my fear. I needed to go to The Rock, and the Holy Spirit went with me.

No One Can Serve Both God and Woman

It's easy to serve God out of a love for someone or something else. Jesus said, *"No man can serve two masters: for either he will hate the one, and love the other; or else he will hold to the one, and despise the other. Ye cannot serve God and mammon"* (Matthew 6:24). Money, fame, love for another, feeling spiritual, and being in control are all slave masters that can steal our services rendered in God's name and make them work against us.

We must serve God out of a love for Him and nothing else. God knew that if I stayed with Tiffany I would never give my heart to Him, so He allowed me to be separated from her. I am not suggesting that God is involved in breaking up marriages or anything of that nature, but I do believe

He removes idols from our lives, no matter how painful, if it means saving our soul.

What motivates you to follow God? Is it power? Is it admiration from others? Why do you call yourself a Christian? Because it's what you've grown up with? Because it's the right thing to do? Why do you do anything spiritual? If the answer is anything but a love for Jesus and a heart to reach the lost, then you are serving two masters. One of them has to go. Make the decision to serve God because you love Him, and nothing else.

Chapter 6

Conversion

In a moment of decision, the best thing you can do is the right thing to do. The worst thing you can do is nothing (Theodore Roosevelt).

"Is there anyone here tonight who doesn't know Jesus? If you don't know the Lord, why don't you come down to the altar and give yourself to Him."

I stood in the back row of the bleachers at The Rock. Alone. Terrified. I fought against raising my hands in worship with "these people," and the urge to go down to the altar.

I had arrived at that night's service in a daze. I had never attended on my own, not without the only person I knew there, not without making fun of a church I felt was inadequate. Now the church I thought was beneath me was in a position to save me, because it offered something I had never had.

Sweet Surrender

The service that night was all music, save for Pastor Steve interjecting what he felt the Holy Spirit had impressed him to say. Raised hands and singing surrounded me.

Everything temporal and eternal rested on my answer to the pastor's question and the feeling in my heart. My decision would decide whether I'd be lost or found. I had reached the most important point of decision a person will have, and when you sense the loving presence of Jesus Christ surrounding you, overpowering you, and beckoning to you, only one decision will really do.

Before I could muster a critical thought, Christ spoke to my heart. I'm sure this isn't a proper transcript, but I felt God saying to me, "Just shut up. Raise your hands, and give it up."

So I did.

It felt like fire. I know that's cliché (especially among Pentecostals who build sermons and worship around the word "fire"). I don't mean a literal burning sensation, like the morning after a late-night Taco Bell binge. I mean the emotional response to realizing just how sinful a creature you really are.

My pride, my resistance to God, my compromise—all lay before my mind's eye. I saw how hollow my religious life really was. My heart burned with sorrow, and I wanted rid of it all. My heart needed to vomit sin. After singing through the worship song, my hands outstretched to heaven, I slowly crept down the bleachers, past worshipers, past onlookers, and past my spiritual pride. I buried my face in the stairs by the altar and responded with my heart. And for the first time in my life, I truly worshipped God.

I suppose it was 25 minutes before I looked up and around the room. The music still played and people were in their own worlds of worship. People were more focused on singing, worshiping, and praying than on whoever came up front that night. Those of us who came down were not the center of attention—God was. I felt cloaked in God's Spirit and safe in the company of these believers. No one cared whether you wanted to cry, shout, or just kneel at the altar for the next hour.

"Where the Spirit of the Lord is, there is freedom" (2 Corinthians 3:17, NIV).

I was free to worship how I needed to. There was no fear of upsetting the status quo. It didn't seem to exist here. I could focus on God without the fear of others focusing on me. It was a strange combination—feeling alone, yet surrounded by the love of God and His followers.

At 9:15 the service began to wind down. I noticed Tiffany laughing in the back row among some of the "spiritually elite." I knew her well enough to tell that it was fake. I realized how she was struggling. She wanted to follow Jesus, but still tiptoed on the fence. I resolved to maintain a genuine faith.

God, I prayed. *One year from now I will know more people than her, I will be involved more than her, and it will be real.* My prayer was audacious, but I was sick of sin. I was sick of weak faith. I was sick of living a meaningless life. I was sick of seeing people fake their Christianity. I was determined to never just fake it, but to turn the tables and make my adversary the devil "who walks around like a roaring lion, seeking whom he may devour" get indigestion at the very thought of eating something of mine.

New Convert

I spent my first few weeks as a new convert calling every heathen friend I ever had and taking them on a walk. I preached the gospel to them and even got one to go back to church. I was on fire. I broke and threw out all my CDs. I was on a roll. But one obstacle still remained.

My relationship with Tiffany took a new twist. When we had stopped dating she seemed to view me as so unspiritual that she couldn't even accept a ride to church from me. You can imagine my surprise when she called, wondering if her "best friend" could pick her up from church events. I was irritated with the girl, but I still had feelings.

One night I found out she had been smoking and partying. I tried to call her to repentance, only to get snide remarks. I tried to act caring like before, only to have it slammed down by critical comments. The next day she called me as sweetly as ever, like nothing had happened, asking if I could pick her up from a ministry meeting she was involved in, and wanting to know if her "best friend" was available.

"Best friend?" I muttered to myself, angry that I'd just agreed to do her bidding.

Pride and Seek

A routine developed. I'd gone from love of her life, to unspiritual peon, to "best friend." I could have killed her, but I had feelings I couldn't shake. Like one of those flying monkeys in The *Wizard of Oz,* I scrambled to do my mistress's bidding. I knew it was dumb, but I entertained the hope of getting back together.

In the mornings before school Tiffani would find me and recount all her experiences with her new boyfriend Coleman. My best friend Steve (who was equally annoyed with her for doing the same dumb stuff to him) and I would pretend to listen to her. When she left we would rip on Coleman. It gave us a grim feeling of satisfaction.

"Coleman?" I would say. "Isn't that the name of a camp stove?"

"I can't believe he has a last name for a first name!" Steve would respond. True, our insults weren't very clever, but at a pity party, it doesn't matter.

Changes for the Better

Meanwhile I went back to playing with High Praize. I had given up on hanging out with my friends at school, and God was faithful to bring all sorts of new people across my path to replace them.

Deciding to cut my long hair was the biggest turning point. First, I wanted a new image to go along with my new life. Second, because at 130 pounds I wasn't a big guy, and I knew there was a problem when Steve's mom mistook me for a girl one day when she came to pick us up from school.

A new approach to life felt good. I began to think about possibilities, and wondered what God would do with my life. As I walked into The Rock after my haircut, my new friends greeted me with applause. Girls complimented my new 'do. I had to reintroduce myself to a couple people. My attitude shifted as well. I dumped the dark act and began to accept myself, because if Christ could accept me, who was I to argue? And that's when the fun began.

Everyone Must Choose

When I talk with Adventists about when they accepted Christ, many play it off. "Oh, I was brought up in the church," they say. "I didn't really have a conversion experience." It's a terrible answer—and the most common. When a lot of Adventists think of accepting Christ they think of a time when they felt an emotional buzz or were knocked off their horse like Paul. If they haven't experienced something similar, they must have no story to tell.

Don't confuse a conversion *experience* with the *point of decision.* Everyone, Christian or not, will have to make a decision for Christ. What matters is whether you make it before or after the judgment. The Bible says, "Every knee should bow, . . . and every tongue confess that Jesus Christ is Lord" (Phil. 2:10, 11, NIV). Those who decide now will have their names written in the Lamb's book of life. Those who make a decision after the Second Coming are simply acknowledging Jesus before they are stripped from existence. Take the time now to ask yourself if you have made that decision, because once you know you have, there's no doubt the devil can throw at you that will make you question your salvation.

"We are to find the assurance of our acceptance with God in His written promise, not in a happy flight of feeling" (Ellen White, *Signs of the Times,* Apr. 18, 1895).

"For worship to be acceptable, it must be offered in faith and hope, and the life must be in harmony with it. God requires the devotion of heart, mind, soul, and strength" (Ellen White, Letter 143, 1904).

Chapter 7

Power

One of the churches' biggest structural failings is that they keep the back door open. Any pastor involved in traditional evangelism can tell you the difficulty of holding on to new converts. Philip Samaan writes: "But when [a new convert] joins the church . . . we drop him like a hot potato" (*Christ's Way of Reaching People,* p. 45).

Churches must plug people into fellowship. Ellen White writes: "There is wise education given to those newly come to the faith. Teach them by giving them something to do, in some line of spiritual work, that their first love will not die but increase in fervor" (*Evangelism,* p. 356). The Rock shined at this. I had more opportunities for involvement at my fingertips than I had fingernails. They solidified my new commitment to Christ, church, and Christianity. The Rock did all they could to help me establish myself in a living, working faith. I was one hot potato that wasn't going to get dropped.

When we first accept Christ, especially if we weren't brought up Christians, we have the spiritual navigation skills of a Tic-tac. We are excited about salvation and have a bounty of questions, but we haven't developed discernment or maturity. "Like newborn babies, crave pure spiritual milk, so that by it you may grow up in your salvation, now that you have tasted that the Lord is good" (1 Peter 2:2, 3, NIV). It is the church's job to provide that spiritual milk for all the babes that come through the door.

Church growth books talk about a "discipleship" track, which encourages new members to become involved and contributing to the work of God. It kept me focused and it kept me in. I believe that if every church had a formal plan to involve new members, far fewer would wander out the back door.

The Rock's first priority was to solidify teens in a personal relationship with Jesus, and then help them develop personal spiritual power. Many churches fail, not for a lack of good programming, financial support or ideas, but for a lack of genuine spiritual power.

I saw people come to Christ every week, in every meeting, and every event. In three years I saw at least 200 youth accept Jesus as their Savior (and that's not including the services in the main sanctuary). Involving them in service helped them build on their commitment.

Altar Calls

Every service had an altar call. You may roll your eyes and groan at the mention of such a tactic because you've witnessed altar calls gone awry. The typical Adventist altar call occurs after an evangelistic message: "If you want salvation, come forward!" Or perhaps, "If you need to make a commitment to Jesus, come up front."

I think such calls are too open. For example, Brother John, a faithful elder for 135 years, knows for sure that he wants to be saved, so he goes forward. Other faithful Christians think, "If *he* is going up, I know I have to."

So what's the problem with recommitting? Nothing. But you have a problem when all you ever call are saved Christians who only came because it seemed the appropriate thing to do. It virtually eliminates a way to measure your effectiveness in reaching *lost people*. You lose the lost in a sea of the saved.

The other trouble I've seen is that the pastor prays a prayer of commitment *for* respondents, not *with* them. He'll thank the Lord for the souls, ask Him to bless them, encourage them to find a pastor (which is a problem because the pastor usually isn't available to talk at that time, and they have no idea who the pastor is anyway.)

At the end of every message at The Rock, regardless of the topic, the speaker made a call to Christ. The speaker would ask those people who raised their hands to come forward, and reemphasize that he wanted *no one* looking around who wasn't coming down to the front. This was the most exciting time of the service. It always thrilled me to the core, as I strained my hearing over the light music being played, to catch the sound of a soul's rustling clothes, clanking footsteps on the metal bleachers, making their way down to the front.

"I am going to ask you to raise your hand on the count of three. Please, nobody looking around—this is between you and God. If you know Jesus then

I want you praying for those who don't. On the count of three, 1-2-3! . . . Amen, praise the Lord! Come on; get those hands up if you don't know Him. If, God-forbid, you should die tonight and you don't know where you would spend eternity, get your hand up! I'm just going to wait a little longer . . ."

The speaker asked altar call respondents to repeat a prayer after him. It went something like this:

"Father God, I come to you tonight in the name of your Son Jesus Christ. I know I'm a sinner, I know I haven't lived my life right, and I know I need help. So I'm asking you to come into my heart tonight. Forgive me of my sins, give me a new heart, and be Lord of my life. And from this day forward, for the rest of my life, I will serve you and no one else. In Jesus' name, amen."

The speaker announced the new arrivals into the Kingdom as we all whooped and hollered, for "There is rejoicing in the presence of the angels of God over one sinner who repents" (Luke 15:10, NIV). They stood in a row, smiling brightly, though some were scared to death, thinking, *What have I just joined?* For just such people, one more process remained. Pastor Steve encouraged the new believers to follow "Care Pastors" to another room because "We want to give you some materials that give you more information about the decision you've just made, and also to provide you with an opportunity to ask any questions you might have."

The teens received a warm welcome, a Bible, a couple tracts, and an opportunity to be "baptized in the Holy Ghost." This helped keep tabs on visitors and to put a personal touch and some friendly faces on the church, so the

78

new converts would feel welcome coming back.

"Teen pastors" partnered up with new people (of the same gender) to make sure they never sat alone or had no one to talk to. The Call Ministry checked up on youth if they didn't check in for several weeks. If there was a problem a Care Pastor could visit the youth or take them out and try to provide any needed assistance.

Discipleship classes taught basic doctrinal beliefs, and how to *live* like a Christian once you have the truth. Topics ranged from effective prayer, Bible study, and spiritual gifts, to *how* to give and not just *what* to give.

Power-Up

All these factors played into my staying in church, despite not going through the formal program and accepting Christ on my own. Knowing Christ was going to be important. I'd need much spiritual power for discernment as I crept deeper into Pentecostalism. I would see and participate in things I would never have imagined. My approach to Christianity was about to shift so radically that I would nearly forget Adventism.

As I read the Bible more and I opened my heart to new influences, I started accepting my new church family's doctrines and practices. Speaking in tongues, being "slain in the spirit," slaying other people in the spirit, and becoming "drunk in the spirit" found their way into my spiritual repertoire. I was ready for anything they wanted to toss my way—whether a healing, a financial miracle, or even a limp body.

Pride and Seek

As a kid I was dumb enough to lick the top of batteries—and like it. That copper-top zing was such a crazy feeling of energy (and probably explains the permanent cowlick on the back of my head). That battery was full of energy to power toys, appliances, and all sorts of electronic wonders.

Have you taken the time to get charged up before approaching your walk with God? You may have talent, know-how, and even a little faith, but even the most successful Christian needs to take time and reenergize. Jesus took time away from the crowds to rest, and encouraged His followers to do the same. I have heard it said that Adventists don't rest very well. That's funny, considering our Sabbath doctrine. We are always "doing" and challenging others to do more. I've even attended retreats that were busier than a normal work week.

When was the last time you took a spiritual retreat? I'm not talking about a fifteen-minute morning devotion either. When was the last time you went away for a weekend alone and spent some time with God, by yourself, listening to what He has been trying to tell you while the noise of your doing drowned Him out?

Take some time to plug in spiritually. If you are involved in a group at church, see how much time the group spends praying and studying scripture for God's messages versus how much time they spend talking about the weather, sports, or church problems. It will determine the strength and satisfaction of your Christian experience and the effectiveness of any church plans you make.

Acts 1:8 says, *"You will receive power when the Holy Ghost comes on you"* (NIV). It's time to start seeking the Spirit of God.

Chapter 8

Definitely Not Church as Usual

Our services should be intensely interesting (Ellen White, *Testimonies*, vol. 9, p. 233).

I recently asked my Sabbath school class if they could use the spiritual gift of prophecy and predict that day's church service. After their comments, I asked if they were powerful enough to predict the next week, and then the week after that. They hit the nail on the head every time. But that's not the most amazing part.

The most amazing part was that their answers not only predicted the services at their church, but just about every other church in the union as well. Incredible. Our church is a 500-member church with more resources than many smaller churches, yet we follow the same patterns to the letter. We don't maximize our potential for worship.

Welcome, music, opening hymn, prayer, offering, prayer, children's story, music, prayer, sermon, closing hymn, prayer. Give or take a prayer, that probably describes the last church service you attended. While there's nothing wrong with that order, there's nothing sacred about it either.

"Many of our pastors have used the same order of service, made the same announcements, sung the same songs, . . . year after year, decade after decade. . . . History shows that the church has lost its influence through failure to change. . . . Adventist ministers should not be afraid to experiment with new forms of worship" (*Minister's Manuel*, p. 133).

We are all ministers in some form or another. That makes us all responsible for our worship services. After 10 years of the same thing, with no change, no growth, and no inspiration, coming back week after week can be hard. We don't attend church to see a "divine service." We attend to see Jesus and know Him deeper.

A New Church Motto

Living Word's motto is *Definitely Not Church as Usual,* Though I was still learning the idiosyncrasies of my new church and how it functioned, attending church became the most anticipated event of the week. The leaders did everything they could to listen to God during the week so they could shape the service as the senior pastor felt impressed by the Holy Spirit, not how the bulletin mandated it.

The church had the most graphically impressive bulletins I have ever seen, full of pictures, on smooth expensive paper, *and thick!* It outlined everything for the month, and listed small groups, employment opportunities, ministry opportunities, weddings, baby dedications. It told anything you could possible need to know in a multi-thousand-member church—except the service order.

It was the pastors' responsibility to lead, and the lay peoples' responsibility to train and work hard with the pastor so they could be led. This produced a dynamic and living service. Church was alive, growing, and in a state of constant change. You never knew what to expect, and yet, because you always knew that you would never know, you felt comfortable and enjoyed yourself. You never checked the bulletin repeatedly during the service, like checking to see what act is being performed in a play you're attending.

Living Word held two basic types of services. The first was Sunday morning service, a comparatively straightforward event. The others were known as Holy Ghost Meetings, and were like nothing I'd ever encountered.

Getting Ready for Church

You've been there before—waking up Sabbath morning in hopes that you can make it to Sabbath school on time. Not because it's *intensely interesting,* but because it's the right thing to do. It wouldn't be so bad if you were the only one who needed to get ready. But a full house can make Sabbath morning far from restful. In my house you had to make bathroom reservations before bedtime. Growing up, I had three other siblings, and pandemonium ensued as we tried to get bathed, fed, dressed, and out the door before 9 a.m.

My Sunday church had no Sunday school, just two services, 8:30 and

Pride and Seek

10:30 a.m. The mad dashing wasn't because we wanted to look good arriving in time for an hour of passionate and purposeless discussion, but because if you didn't get to church at a decent time you would end up with seats so far away in the balcony you could have a view of the third heaven.

Seat Saving

People arrived at 7 a.m. just to put their Bibles down near the front. People actually enjoyed sitting up front where they could see the speaker, make eye contact, get a smile of approval, and hear every precious Word of life spoken. (Most church members I know wouldn't sit up front if I taped hundred dollar bills to the seats.)

People attended because they expected to hear from God. They didn't want to be distracted by a talkative balcony seat. I think the closest I got on a Sunday morning was fifth row center, and even then I had to sprint to beat out an older gentleman who had been hurdling past other seats. No matter how many times I tried to get second row, I'd see Bibles and journals lying on every single chair I wanted to sit on.

I was always greeted by sharply dressed people wearing name tags. They had nice smiles, firm handshakes, and good breath—which was important because, as Pastor Steve always said, "People should fall out under the power of God, not your breath." They were genuinely happy to see me, even though they didn't know who I was.

Living Word built a new building while I was attending. Massive and elaborately decorated, it boasted hand-painted furniture by Ralph Lauren. A huge crystal chandelier hung from the 30-foot vaulted ceiling. Art depicting the life of Christ hung from the walls. A welcome center waited with volunteers eager to point you to any scrap of information you might need. A bookstore was open before and after service.

The Main Sanctuary

After meeting my friends, we would enter the sanctuary, reserve a seat and chat for a bit while everyone else filtered in. The new sanctuary sat 4,500. Lit up with all sorts of lighting fixtures, it was so bright you would never have noticed there were no windows. The colors were crèmes, blues, purples, and whites. I always stopped for a moment to take in the beauty of God's House. I know as Adventists we preach against extravagance in our buildings, but having visited enough homes, I can't help but wonder—shouldn't God's house be nicer than ours? We sat in theater seating, which I grew to like because it let you know exactly how many people the church could hold, and it kept people's elbows in check. (There's nothing worse than an unexpected elbow acting as a bookmark in your Bible when you are trying to follow a sermon.)

The musicians and choir walked out and the talking ceased as the music erupted. It consisted of a white digital drum set with silver trim, a six-string bass, a guitar, horns, and the music minister, who sat at a black grand piano and welcomed everyone during the introduction to the first song. I began to see why this church had such an appreciation for worship. The music minister trained his people, cast a vision for them, and challenged them to give it their all. As the 100-member choir began singing, the congregation experienced an outpouring of God's presence that only countless hours and preparation can bring.

The music minister sat with the rest of the band on stage right, with four lead singers center stage, and the large choir stage left. The worship leader, Pastor Tim, provided the cues and transitions. The singers and band members followed his lead, playing everything from powerful praise music to melodic, harmony-filled worship songs. The sound guys were expertly trained, so no ear-splitting feedback created a need for an anointing service, and no one musician distracted from the others.

The Worship Experience

We experienced worship in three ways. First, we got to listen and watch. When you listen to Christian music in your car, while you clean, or at the office it uplifts you and keeps you motivated, but its differs greatly in style and talent from what burrows in your ear, lays eggs, and hatches on Sabbath morning.

Secondly, we were taught by example. Pastor Tim exhorted us to follow along with him and participate in the songs. Even if they were new, we learned lickety-split because we were taught. Think of it as VBS for adults. Occasionally Pastor Tim asked us to raise our "holy hands" in surrender. Because it was asked from the front, and the musicians did it, and the pastors did it, the initial weirdness of it left quickly.

Having someone lead out in worship is a concept that some churches practice and others don't for varying reasons. There is certainly a danger of a leader becoming self-absorbed or letting a congregation get carried away with itself in the blaze of high octane worship music, but I believe there is great value in teaching believers how to worship, as well as placing a burden on the musicians to lead their people. People can sense when a real experience with God is desired. At least I could, and so do many other Adventist youth who leave our churches in search of a genuine worship experience.

The third blessing we got was a worshipful atmosphere. I hate to say it, and people will disagree, but worship atmospheres are hard to come by in Adventist churches sometimes. Certainly I'm not referring to experience and, dare I say it, *feeling*—am I? Adventists have become so spooked by emotionalism that we say, "It's not about feeling," or "It's more than experience," every time we want to excuse a poorly planned worship service. We have used that excuse so much that we have virtually eliminated feeling and experience from most worship services. And let me tell you, having seen and experienced emotionalism firsthand, what most SDA churches view as emotionalism is so far away from it that they couldn't discern emotionalism if it came and passed out on their doorstep.

I experienced worship as an experience. It was a safe haven to express worship to God, feel His presence, hear His voice, and experience His reality in such a way that you wanted to shout to the world, "He's real!" As the music played you could sing along, sit down, pray, kneel, raise hands, weep, or pass out. It was between you and God. The music and the singing was loud enough that you wouldn't feel embarrassed if you sang off key, or shouted hallelujah, and yet it wasn't so loud it hurt your ears.

As the music drifted into mellow worship hymns and then drifted again into instrumental selections, the pastor would walk on stage and begin praying. He didn't need to announce it was time to pray, for we were already in a worshipful and prayerful attitude. He encouraged us to stretch out our hands to God and believe in His blessing in the service. After prayer the musicians left and our pastor greeted us with a warm smile and welcome. The service transitioned as smoothly as a greased pig.

Keeping the Flow Going

The whole service was like that. Smooth. Streamlined. No dead air, microphone fumbling, or people looking around panicked because they don't know where they're supposed to be. Deacons didn't need to be called forward, they just knew. It was orderly, and I praised God for it. The spirit of worship was never broken, because they took great care to keep the flow going.

I hate choppy church. The Sabbath is a time to worship God and give Him our best, and yet people are so reluctant to commit any time to practice and develop a service that we end up with something half-baked. We wouldn't do a presentation at our jobs with only an hour of prep time, so why do it with the Gospel?

After the offering the senior pastor reviewed what he had previously preached on, which made us feel as if we were going somewhere. The sermons lasted about an hour. That's an obscene amount of time for most people. However, what most people don't hear or expect is a teaching (not a sermon) that, if followed, will bring blessing and peace into their life as soon as they leave church and put it into practice. The pastor's sermons were readily applicable and the majority of people brought journals and notebooks to church to take notes. Churches usually have to give away notes on the sermon. Sermons were challenging and positive, and I felt better for having come.

Church always ended with an altar call. They firmly believed and instilled in us that every service might be someone's last chance to accept Christ. Folks usually came forward and when they did, members of the volunteer staff called altar counselors were ready to receive them, pray with them, and give them any information they might need.

Big churches you see might not have all the truth we enjoy, but they often have more dedication to serving God. They put hours and hours in just to make sure visitors don't leave without receiving something from God. What's holding you back from throwing every inch of your being into the work of God? Where is your enthusiasm for the miracles God wants to work in us and for us daily? Young adults and youth, is it more important to complain or to do something about it? You are called to leadership—it's time to step up.

To even be a volunteer or hold a position at Living Word you had to take a leadership class. To become a member you had to attend classes, and you had to be 18 so you could understand the weight and responsibility of what you were getting into. To be allowed on stage you had to spend weeks behind the scenes, learning how everything worked so you (and the congregation) could have a good experience.

Growing up, people made it seem like Adventists were the only ones who practiced healthy and spiritual living. Wrong. In many ways they had higher standards than we do, and yet they had no factions complaining about having to live the Christian life. The difference was how they communicated their standards. They did it in to inspire greatness; we tend to do it in a way that promotes discouragement. We want obedience; they sought to empower you. "When Christ spoke to the disciples of the Holy Spirit, He sought to uplift their thoughts and enlarge their expectations to grasp the highest conception of excellence" (*This Day with God,* p. 257). When Jesus calls His people to greater understanding it is to lift them higher, not to force them into lifeless duty. I want to see the bar raised.

The Spirit of Sunday

Of all the new doctrines I encountered, and of all the new ideas I tried on for size, going to church on Sunday was the easiest for me to get used to. It only bothered me when someone referred to it as the Lord's day. Sunday morning services were the tamest of all services. Sure, things were dynamic, but not wild, with acts of enthusiasm limited to clapping and whistling. This was intentional, because most visitors came to that service.

While there was structure and a specific vision communicated that Sunday mornings were to be more of a teaching time, the break in monotony came in the fact that pastors could change things up mid-service. We might sing for 30 minutes, or five. We might pray in the middle of the sermon, have multiple preachers share things on the spot, or hear a sermon the pastor had felt impressed to preach while sitting during music. The senior pastor told us that he had only preached the same sermon two or three times in his 20+ years in ministry. There was no fear of "old manna."

There were also frequent guest speakers Sunday morning, as well as evangelistic services called Open House weekend, where unchurched friends could hear the basic gospel message, get some free stuff, and get a tour of the $23 million facility. But, as exciting as those were, they were nothing compared to Holy Ghost meetings. Holy Ghost meetings were the equivalent to an emotional, spiritual, and mental nuclear warhead detonation. And as my luck would have it as a visitor, my first experience wasn't on a Sunday morning. Nope. I had my baptism by fire.

Holy Ghost Meetings

These special meetings happened Sunday night, Wednesday night, during stewardship meetings, and special weekend services with guest speakers who had "the anointing." The mind-set behind it all was, "We're going to let the Spirit of God do what it wants." At least that's what I heard during opening prayer my first time attending the adult church. I had no idea what all the Holy Ghost liked to do. Maybe sing some songs? Read the Bible? Have testimonies? Pray? Have a bake sale?

Pride and Seek

"The anointing" is a term charismatics use to designate the power and gifts of the Holy Spirit. This phrase is used more frequently than people breathe. It's assigned to anyone who demonstrates a gift or ability. For example, "The Pastor is anointed to preach," or, "That worship music was anointed." Ministers and lay leaders are regarded as having high quantities of the anointing and can be considered as apostles and even prophets. Seems like a simple concept, right? It would be, if this was the only way this term was used.

Charismatics believe that the Holy Ghost moves in its power in every service, and not just through people. Where "the anointing" becomes confusing is when it is assigned to inanimate objects or to certain parts of the room. For example: "The anointing is moving around the room," or when the anointing has character traits: "There is an anointing of healing in this place." Usually, if the anointing is moving around, it can trigger all sorts of craziness. People will laugh uncontrollably, pass out, or dance. It is confusing when you first encounter it because when someone says, "The anointing is over there!" and you look and see nothing, you begin to wonder about the sanity of your brothers and sisters in the Lord. The anointing is also used interchangeably with "the spirit."

When the anointing is moving, it is often referred to as "waves." I watched many friends who were walking upright, only to double over, breathe deeply, and inform me that they'd just "caught a wave." The wave's effect is numerous. Since the spirit is likened to a river at times, you will hear people talk about getting in "the flow," and thereby catching a "wave." Just think of it as spiritual surfing.

It's not to say there wasn't structure. There was. Ushers stood by in case someone got unruly, catchers were ready for people who got slain in the spirit, and pastors waited in the wings in case they needed more hands on deck for any potential shipwreck. The music was less inhibited, meaning that one song could go for an hour, or any singer could sing words that had previously not been a part of any song in existence up until that point.

My first HG meeting featured an evangelist named Rodney Howard Browne. As I sat down on the left side of the stage I observed the kinetic excitement my fellow churchgoers were trying to contain. They quivered like lab rats awaiting a caffeine fix. The service proceeded like normal until the preaching started. Those attending said it was the anointing, but I thought it could be a medical condition because right in the middle of a presentation by Pastor Browne's wife, Pastor Browne started giggling. She would pause, and he would excuse himself with great difficulty, only to begin sniggering again when she started. Was her fly down or something?

I was really curious and scooted to the edge of my seat to observe this bizarre occurrence. His laughing got louder and more frequent. People began to cheer and clap mildly in response. People told me the *anointing* was having a *manifestation;* and I wondered if that meant Browne had food poisoning, or if his wife had a known flatulence problem. I had no idea what people were talking about. The laughter continued until he had control of the mic again. By now the church was buzzing with expectancy. He went into a talk about the fire of God and how the Spirit was being poured out, and people began to whoop and holler.

Soon all heaven broke loose . . . I guess. Pastor Browne began screaming and yelling "FIRE!", stretching his hands out over sections of the audience. People in those sections flew back into their seats and, well, either twitched or passed out. Pastor Browne went all around the church like a wizard casting a spell. I was so enthralled at this spectacle that I didn't notice that he was making his way around to my section! I also didn't consider the irony of if there had actually been a physical fire in the building, and he was really trying to warn us of impending doom, only to have us drop like flies.

I went into a brief panic. What was going to happen? Was the Spirit really expelling some tangible heat? Would I go out cold? Was I going to twitch? Sure enough, his fire yelling came around. I grew tense. I sat there, not breathing. Ready, set, FIRE!

Instantly, everyone around me flew against the back of their seats, laughing, passing out, or twitching. Except me. I had squinted as the pastor came around, readying myself for impact, only to feel nothing. However, upon noticing everyone around me feeling something, I felt I had better do something so I wouldn't look conspicuous. It might have been a delayed reaction, but I passed out just as good as the rest of them. Eventually I opened my eyes as everyone else was getting up.

Holy laughter was erupting all over the place. Uncontrollable bursts of joy. People laughed, fell over, and squirmed around. The most bizarre was when Pastor Browne looked into the balcony and saw a woman standing up, to which he yelled, "Get her Lord! Just get her!"

The woman began laughing, then doubled over, and eventually fell over backward (thankfully the spirit didn't move her over the edge of the balcony). The same happened to others as well. I don't even remember what the sermon was about, I was so intent on watching the display of emotionalism. I had seen a little of this at The Rock, but never to this degree. I just sat there thinking, *These people are crazy! I can't believe what I'm seeing.* I had no intention of participating, save warming my seat, at this stage in my charismatic experience, but after attending these meetings for a year, my spiritual journey landed me in the stead of the annual stewardship meetings. It was here I couldn't resist jumping into the fray.

Glory Run

Each year during the stewardship campaign the pastor preached on the vision for the upcoming year. A string of special guests (with the anointing!) came and psyched everyone up to participate. Every year the speakers get more excited, the vision gets bigger, and people's expectancy rises, but the year I attended was extra special. They had just moved into their new facility, and now they needed to give like they had never given before to pay for it.

They promised financial breakthroughs, if we would only give. A stream of promotions around the church advertised such miracles of God as healing, vision, and peace. The hype took me by storm. I had to go.

As a young Adventist I was taught to never run in the church sanctuary.

Pride and Seek

Pathfinders even has kids recite "walk softly in the sanctuary" in their official pledge. You can imagine my surprise the first time I encountered a glory run.

One Sunday evening I was almost run over by a human freight train barreling through the church, shouting praises. *Whoa! That was crazy,* I thought. *I wonder how many times that will happen tonight?* That night's speaker oozed anointing, and people just could not sit still.

Sitting in the balcony with my friends, I watched as several people suddenly got excited and jumped up to start running. The speaker hadn't done anything exciting either, as he was preaching a very straightforward message. But soon about ten people were up running, and the pastor got excited because running meant the Spirit was moving. "If you're feeling the same Spirit," he said, "just get up and run."

Just get up and run?

I stared, transfixed, as 2000 people frolicked around a church sanctuary—the elderly, the juvenile, and the sophisticated bounding across seats, stage, stairs, and floral arrangements. I had no idea how to respond. So I ran.

I felt a rush of freedom as I broke childhood rules. I had permission to run in church—from the pastor! I would actually be looked down upon if *I didn't.* I felt a rush of immature glee as I joined the conga line chugging down the stairs of this multi-million dollar sanctuary. My brothers and sisters and I stampeded over the stage, on national television! I turned and waved at the camera, thinking, *I can't believe I'm doing this!*

Round and round we went, people cheering us on. I made three laps before I sat down again. It was a spiritual marathon, and since I was pretty quick, it looked as if I would win the gold medal for church sprints. I seriously considered doing a back flip down front. I remember staring into the bright stage lights—the same stage that famous pastors preached on, that thousands of viewers turned in to see, and that allowed me to look over at hundreds of empty seats and think, *What on earth are we doing?*

Even after I sat down a few dedicated sprinters remained. A couple of them almost ran over the pastor.

Downright Bizarre

As I sat back down in my balcony seat next to my friend Brian we noticed the woman. Brian had been my close buddy for two years now, and we enjoyed the same off the wall humor, so we were glad the other was there when we saw the Spirit move again. A woman in her 40s had run up to the pastor and begun hopping/jogging in circles around him, singing praises and waving her hands in the air. Brian and I laughed heartily—but Brian stopped laughing when I leaned in and made an important discovery:

"Dude, that's your mom!"

"Oh, no," Brian groaned, clapping his hands over his face.

As the pastor tried to get back to the sermon, another spiritual blessing greeted him: a holy roller. I was familiar with the term, but had never actually considered what they were.

The minister had decided to stand down front at the end of the center aisle. The cheering we had heard only moments before when Brian's mom did her little dance started up again. I am sure the preacher stopped his sermon instinctively after almost being knocked over by runners earlier. The worshiper would not be as threatening this time, just more disturbing.

Tucked into a tight ball, coming from origins I couldn't see, a young man rolled his way up to the front. Clapping ensued as he made his pilgrimage ever closer to the minister. The ushers stood ready and waiting. But there was no need. Upon reaching the feet of the minister, the gentleman quietly backward-rolled to his seat to the delight of the congregation. The meetings went on like this for a few weeks, save Sunday mornings.

Some Positives

I tried not to miss many Holy Ghost meetings, because good preachers who delivered messages that, despite distractions, I still remember. I didn't want to miss anything good and have to hear it secondhand the next day. For example, on leave from college once, I visited a Sunday morning service. One of my old friends ran up to me and asked if I had been at the previous night's service. I hadn't, but I found out what I missed. The senior pastor had done a superman dive off the stage into the second row of chairs landing on the associate pastor and his wife.

As crazy as it all sounds, there were limits. I gained incredible respect for the senior pastor during one Holy Ghost meeting, when some of the leadership did a loud and obnoxious ring-around-the-rosy "in the spirit" just off stage right. The senior pastor took the stage and broke up the antics. "It's okay to express your joy and faith," he said, "but we are not exhibitionists." The meeting ended peacefully. I was wowed. I never thought I would see such a quick rebuke, and I admire the pastor for it, because no one would have objected if he had let it go on.

I still value certain elements of the Holy Ghost meetings: the unwillingness to be bound by a program or structure; the refusal to worship a service order; the openness to spontaneity. I appreciated the element of surprise, and even if it got out of control, it was joyful. I never left church feeling worse than when I walked in.

Purposefully Peculiar

1 Peter 2:9 (KJV) says: *"But ye are a chosen generation, a royal priesthood, an holy nation, a **peculiar** people; that ye should shew forth the praises of him who hath called you out of darkness into his marvellous light."* The word the KJV translates as "peculiar" is *peripoasin,* which means "a possession." A lot of people take the idea of being unique and chosen for God and turn it into a martyr complex. We excuse weak evangelism numbers on our peculiar doctrines and our way of doing church. Our status as "the Remnant" somehow explains away our ineffective witnessing to the local community. Some people consider any alteration of "the way we've always done it" as a blatant departure from our call to be distinctive. There's a mix-up, because that type of peculiarity is obsessed with *how people look at us,* instead of *how we approach people.*

Pride and Seek

Living Word wanted to be peculiar from the world, but not for peculiarity's sake. They wanted to give people who were disillusioned with church and Christians a refreshing biblical perspective. They wanted people to experience God in a way they didn't know was possible. They wanted to be peculiar for a purpose.

How are you "peculiar"? How do you stand out from how others Christians act, speak, or think? How does your church view being peculiar? Is it an opportunity to clarify your community's stereotypes of what Christians are all about, or is it to perpetuate an exclusiveness? Ask yourself, and then adjust your peculiarity to be a purposeful weapon against the enemy. Reach out and change peoples' thinking about God. I am in church today because a church showed me my God in a peculiar way.

"Is it not your duty to put some skill and study and planning into the matter of conducting religious meetings—how they shall be conducted so as to do the greatest amount of good, and leave the very best impression upon all who attend?" (Ellen White, *Review and Herald,* April 14, 1885).

Chapter 9

New Perspective on Ministry

"Preaching the Gospel of Jesus Christ is the highest privilege and the most fascinating adventure ever given to humankind" (*Minister's Manual*, p. 17).

"God is to be praised with the voice and the heart should go therewith in holy exultation" (Charles Spurgeon).

"The highest of all work is ministry in its various lines, and it should be kept before the youth that there is no work more blessed of God than that of the gospel minister" (Ellen White, *Testimonies*, vol. 6, p. 411).

Before I became an Adventist minister I had a less than orthodox (and less than ethical) career as a classroom evangelist. In fifth grade my best friend Steve and I would crawl the walls with boredom in English class. As exciting as grammar was, it just didn't seem to fit the bill for engaging mental stimulation, so we sought out a form of activity better suited to our needs. Inspired by televangelists, we turned to "evangelizing" our classmates.

When our teacher would leave the room for more than two minutes the spirit would begin to move. I would look over my shoulder across the classroom and say, "I feel a healing coming on!" Kids began to smile. They knew it was time for a blessing. "Brother Steve," I queried, "do you feel a healing coming on?"

"Oh, yes, Pastor Pierce, I can feel it!"

I sprang up from my chair, made my way across the swamp green carpet, and swept the perimeter of the classroom.

"Is there *some*body who needs a healing in this room, Brother Steve?"

"Oh, yes, Pastor Pierce, I can feel it!"

After going back and forth for a few moments psyching up the class, we would find ourselves at the desk of a less-than-popular kid.

Raising our hands in the air, while Jerry closed his eyes, mumbling curses under his breath, we "laid hands on him," usually upside the head; sometimes downside. Any side, really, worked for us, and while giving the kid a good whack, we would yell, "Demons, be gone!" Naturally he yelled at us, making all sorts of threats that we knew would never come to fruition. We danced around, telling the class how we had "exorcised the demons."

The cruel irony to all this mayhem was that we always managed to get back to our seats and our studies before the teacher returned. The only one still making noise was our victim, whom she promptly told to be quiet because she could hear him out in the hall, and if he wanted to end up in the principal's office, he should just keep it up.

Ministry was never a career option for me—it was something to make fun of. I was into baseball, movies, and business ventures making millions, not preaching, suits, and visiting hospitals. It seemed pretty bland, and given the persona of televangelists, pretty cheesy. I never thought it would play a role in developing me as a person.

As far as I could tell, ministry was not too different from my classroom revivals. There's a lot of noise, people get hurt, and nothing gets accomplished. I had seen a great deal of churches with fantastic new ministry ideas but no follow through, and I had seen expensive evangelistic series with no follow up. I saw ministers ill-prepared to handle the frustrations of the Christian life, or the frustration of other Christians. I saw disappointment, hurt, and people making minimal results out to be incredible breakthroughs in ministry.

Many pastors also looked at the ministry as such impoverished drudgery that it could only be tolerable if you were called by God and willing to suffer the agonies of cheap clothing, no vacations, no family time, and driving a Yugo. No thanks.

I sensed a difference at Living Word. I saw purposeful, goal-oriented, streamlined ministry. I saw ministers who loved their jobs and operated with spiritual power and influence to achieve their Godly dreams and goals. It made Christianity out to be the most exciting, worthwhile activity possible. Sure they had difficulties and struggles, but why focus on them? Just deal with them and move on. It smashed my preconceived ideas about what ministry was all about, and illuminated my mind to the possibilities of being involved at church. It drew me in, and soon my life was ministry.

Pride and Seek

High Praize

My fingers oozed sweat as I stood fiddling with my guitar strings. Being on stage playing guitar with a band at top volume was a fantasy I wasn't quite ready for when it came into reality. The blue and red lights illuminated the stage and the other musicians, who were used to this sort of thing. They knew the drill. While they calmly waited for the worship leader's signal, I was a mess of nerves and anticipation. I didn't even think my body would allow me the coordination of putting on my guitar strap before the first song began.

When I did manage to get my guitar in the ready position I had a panic attack in my heart as I looked out over 200 anxious youth wanting to praise the Lord. What if I messed up? What if they couldn't hear me? It was my first solo performance, and the wait to begin was killing me.

Truthfully, I probably only waited 15 seconds or so before the leader gave the signal and the drums kicked in with a fast rhythm that made everyone cheer and stand on their feet. The clapping started just as quick, and the nervousness melted into excitement as my instruments' turn came. I struck a chord, people responded, and I was instantly ready to praise the Lord.

The first song we did was a number that you will only here in a charismatic church. It's not that you haven't heard the title of the song, or even the melody; it's the fact that we played the 15-minute extended remix version. Charismatics are known for this. They play a song, the spirit moves, and we worship "until the Lord tells us to stop."

Faster and faster we flew in the song, repeating the chorus over and over to more and more excited worshipers. It was quite a contrast to what I was used to. Here, people would come down front smiling and dancing to the music, and if we wanted to punish them, we would threaten to stop. People sang for the 15 minutes! At one point I looked over at Fred the drummer and the poor guy was sweating like he was in a sauna. The singers kept going, and all around the Rockatorium, people were laughing, leaping, singing, and weeping. I was so taken with the sight I almost forgot to bring it down a notch as we went into our more worshipful arrangements.

The music transitioned from driving beats into mellow choruses, accented by the dimming lights. The guitar part became easier, Fred got a rest, and the emphasis moved from the technique of our instruments to the vocal power of our singers. They sang with a passion that spoke to sleepy hearts and created a beautiful invitation for the presence of God. People knelt and prayed, confessed sins, cried, or simply swayed back and forth with hands and voices lifted. Everyone was focused on God at this point, and if we had decided to keep on playing for another 40 minutes, no one would have noticed. They were enamored with the spirit.

As we gradually grew softer in volume the pastor hopped on stage and gave opening prayer while everything was quiet and reverent. Once he was finished we exited, only to return at the end of the sermon to provide some ambiance for the altar call and closing prayer. Lightly played music during opening and closing prayer added to seamless transitions in service and held our focus on worship.

Pride and Seek

The highlight of my time with High Praize was when they decided to record a live CD. My high school was home to at least 194 failed attempts at starting a garage band and producing a CD, and now that I had found the Lord, the opportunity presented itself. I would have my name on the sleeve of an album cover! Even if it only sold 3 copies, my name was in print!

As rewarding as it was, I didn't stay with High Praize for long. I had disagreements and competition with the veteran guitar player in the group. We had different personalities and guitar styles. After he refused to teach me the chords to a song, I resigned and pursued another ministry, one that would establish me as a leader and a presence in the youth group.

The Element of Surprise

The Rock wanted something that would break the ice for visitors, entertain those who had memories of church being dry and boring, and still offer spiritual themes pointing in the right direction. The Rock had a Sunday night program specifically geared for unchurched people, and the pastor needed something within a structure that had a certain level of unpredictability to keep people awake. Enter Streetlight Drama, stocked with people unafraid to look like a fool for the Lord. Because we wrote a lot of our own skits, we could incorporate inside jokes, hidden talents, and have free creative reign (as long as it wasn't sacrilegious) over what was performed.

Characters in our skits included Kung Fu Johnny, who leapt into Ninja action when a young person was tempted by the devil, and Bibleman, the same premise with the addition of a cheesy voice. There was also The Sheep. A leftover prop from a Christmas play, it was a wooden frame adorned with cotton balls, and we snuck it into every skit we possibly could. It appeared in people's backpacks, under tables, in the dialogue, and was once even beheaded (by accident).

Our "icebreakers," performed once or twice a month, had no spiritual value. In one skit, Nick (six feet three, 215 pounds, all muscle) dressed in tight 70s clothes and lip synched *Disco Inferno*. Another time we did a Richard Simmons style "Spiritual Aerobics" routine to warm up the church. (I don't suggest you try it Sabbath morning.)

There were serious performances though as well. We covered topics like depression, family abuse, and suicidal thoughts in dramatic monologues and mime skits set to Christian music. We also did evangelistic skits portraying the battle between God and Satan. My very first skit was called The Champion (set to Carmen's song "The Champion") and was a dramatic mime skit.

I played Jesus. I wore an all white costume, and had about three practices to perfect a choreographed fight sequence. I would perform it twice that night because they had two Sunday night services. I basked in the glow of superstardom at practices, but like my first performance with High Praize, my acting debut was filled with more queasiness and panic.

As I waited in the wings, the floodlights went out and the music started. The devil and his demons emerged from the opposite side of the stage. Snarling and lashing out at the crowd, they wore all black, their faces glowing green under the black lights. Laughing, the devil whirled his dark cloak about himself. The music shifted, lights flickered, and the devil cringed. It was my cue.

I burst onto stage followed by a string of angels in white, throwing glitter out of our hands, which created a shimmering effect around us. I couldn't believe the adrenaline rush. People cheered for Jesus, and I was suddenly taken with the role I was playing. I felt unworthy. My palms sweated as my mind's eye looked forward to the victorious end of the skit.

People clapped and cheered at the end. The feeling was electrifying. I did it! I was center stage, serving the Lord, and being recognized for it. I was a success, and people were pleased with what I could do. At last my identity began to truly take shape. I belonged at church, and I was meant to be in God's family.

Teenpastors

The final ministry I became involved with was the Teenpastor program. Taking its vision from 2 Timothy 4:12, we were taught never to let anyone underestimate what God can do through a youth who has dedicated their life to God. We were taught that youth must set the example of excellent service to God and man. We had a pledge and values that we strove to uphold. Teenpastors were the glue and the leadership among the youth, and played perhaps the most vital role in reaching kids for Christ. We also got neat t-shirts.

After about a year and a half of attendance I was established as a regular in the drama ministry and still had a good relationship with people from High Praize. By now I had more friends than I had ever had, and since public school couldn't offer me any programs to lift my soul, I wanted to spend as much time at The Rock as possible. What better way than to join another ministry? And since I was becoming a leader in the youth group, I felt the need for more training and experience.

Teenpastors involved some 70 youth members. Four teams of 8-10 people, with a youth leader and assistant leader, took responsibility for designated meetings each week. A potential Teenpastor had to interview with two people and demonstrate spiritual maturity.

The Teenpastor ministry consisted of spiritually mature youth who could serve on a basic level of pastoral ministry. Activities ranged from preaching (once every other month), teaching discipleship classes for youth who wanted to be involved in ministry, simply hanging around to answer questions ("Where's the bathroom?"), to offering spiritual support (such as catching people who were slain in the spirit). We were the support staff to the adults.

The Teenpastor Conference

The duties were rewarding and fun, but the best part was the professional growth provided for us. The biggest was the year-end Teenpastor conference and banquet. Each summer's event lasted for two-and-a-half days. The church booked 100 rooms at a fancy hotel, brought in a special speaker, rented out conference rooms, provided meals, and catered a banquet to say farewell to high school seniors leaving The Rock and to welcome in new recruits.

The conference started with breakfast Sunday. Melvin, the leader for the

Teenpastor ministry, welcomed us and lead the first few sessions. Melvin was a nurse who worked third shift, and rarely slept because he was the head of a ministry consisting of over 100 people that required as much time as another full-time job. And he did it with excellence.

After several hours Pastor Munds arrived full of energy, communicating in a way that made us laugh, reinvigorating our souls. We needed it after sitting for hours on end on hard bleachers. After that we hopped into our cars and drove the half mile to the hotel.

The hotel wasn't a cut the corners, bare bones closet. We were guests and workers for the church, and they went out of their way to make sure we knew we were appreciated. Even if we were only teenage volunteers, we entered that place like CEOs. Mother Teresa said, "There is more hunger for love and appreciation in this world than for bread." We never went without it at The Rock.

The lobby had beautiful floors, contemporary furniture and design, and a marvelous section with a pianist playing a glossy blank grand piano. Live music echoed through the hotel as we checked in and boarded the glass elevators. The lobby grew smaller and smaller as we glided up to our rooms.

Our first appointment was at the Mall of America. Our task was to compete with other teams in taking the most creative picture. We dined out on the town, simply enjoying an evening of Christian fellowship.

The next morning we had special meetings with our guest speaker. But before every session, and during the breaks, little carts waited outside the conference rooms, filled with cookies, muffins, cereal, fruit, pop, juice, and the most beloved of all snacks, ice cream bars. There is an urban legend that I once snuck 14 bars into a meeting and ate them all. That is simply not true. I suppose it could have been around five, but that is hardly anything to get excited about. Nonetheless, a "one bar per meeting" rule was enacted after I graduated.

We ended our conference with a banquet. It was a miracle that anyone got ready, considering there were 100 teenagers vying for bathroom time and seeking each other out to borrow belts, socks, ties, and deodorant.

The banquets somewhat resembled a high school graduation, with pictures shown and each senior thanking those who helped them and sharing some of their plans for the future. Several awards were given as well—for team of the year, the ministry of excellence award, and Teenpastor of the year.

The Right Perspective

Ellen White wrote, "With such an army of workers as our youth, rightly trained, might furnish, how soon the message of a crucified, risen, and soon-coming Saviour might be carried to the whole world!" (*Education,* p. 271). My time with Teenpastors gave me a taste of ministry, including an opportunity to preach. They truly recognized the value in preparing and training youth for the work of the church by going beyond fund-raisers, feeding the homeless, and getting badges in Pathfinders. They also recognized the value in appreciating the people who volunteered their resources to make the church a success.

I'm a pastor today thanks to all these opportunities for involvement. I discovered that ministry works, ministry is rewarding, and ministry is worth it.

Pastors often dwell on the negative, from songs we dislike, past failures, people who don't listen to us, and church structure, all the way down to how much denominational workers get paid. It bothers me. It bothers me, especially when I catch myself doing it. Every time I act irritated with the work, joke about my salary, and even give an ear to embittered ministers, I am sending a message to people who might be searching for a call from God. It's a message that says it would be far better for you to tie a millstone around your neck than work as a full-time minister. In my opinion, it's a sin to harbor such an attitude.

Guess what? Ministry is fun. Ministry pays a good salary with good benefits. Ministry changes people's lives. Ministry challenges you to become a better person. Ministry has limitless potential. Ministry lets you meet new people. Ministry is an honor. And for those who always seem to be struggling with three church districts, labeling the church as "dead," spreading woes about their life, grumbling about conferences, being critical of everything, ministry is a calling. And if you're not called to it, then you won't be able to stand it.

You want to hear something scary? You want to know why some churches have explosive growth? You want to know why their sermons are deeper and more effective than so many of ours? It's because they have a larger focus on Christ's return than we do. Everything they do is in light of going to heaven, and living in a powerful way for God to influence others to make a decision for eternity. They believe God will bring results no matter what. They believe that when Jesus said, "I will make you fishers of men," He really meant it.

I remember sitting in a chapel at Oral Roberts University (when I thought I was going to be a charismatic minister). A leader called out, "Are you rapture ready?" Everyone sprang up out of their seat into the air as if they were being "caught up." Silly, eh? But they're ready for what they believe will happen. Are we? Are we ready to serve God with a ready spirit? Are we ready to bless ministry in all its forms and know that God will bring the harvest?

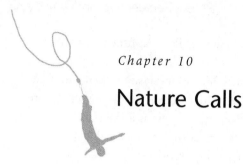

Chapter 10

Nature Calls

Those who dwell, as scientists or laymen, among the beauties and mysteries of the earth are never alone or weary of life (Rachel Carson).

Four-thirty a.m. is a devilish hour—at least when you're forced to wake up so you can sit on a Greyhound bus for 10 hours. It was time for camporee, that whimsical time where young pioneers from all over the union converge on one spot to wrestle with nature—or at least get lost in it.

I barely found my way onto the rumbling bus because my eyes had shut involuntarily. I made my way to an empty section of seats and plopped down my pillow, followed by my body. I desired precious slumber. Steve Lauer, who normally shared the same disruptive and hyperactive behavior as I did, sat next to me. He wasn't sleepy at all. He was wide awake and intensely interested in making me the same. He succeeded.

We tried singing that old song *99 Bottles of Beer on the Wall* to pass the endless miles to Missouri. Our youth pastor pleaded with us to use a different beverage. We merrily obliged and sang *99 Bottles of Coke on the Wall.* Apparently this didn't sit with the health message either, and yet again we were forced to change our tune. We tried milk. No good.

"How about water?" he suggested. We gave up. Obviously this man had never known what it was like to be under the age of 80.

Upon arrival at our campsite, we set up, and had a look around. The area was pretty enough, and there was a great river for swimming not too far away. The sun shone and being able to run after such an obnoxious ride was liberating. Things were looking up. Until the rain fell.

It rained the whole stinking time. Mud was everywhere. It was caked all over us. The fun events were canceled. The food was cold. We were cold. We couldn't escape the moisture that permeated our sleeping bags and tent walls, and seeing that dryness was futile, our pastor suggested an endurance hike. *Sure,* I thought. *This trip can't get any dumber.*

The hike took us through mud and woodland trails, which normally would have been fun if we would have had a place to clean up or get dry. Then came the unbelievable. As we arrived at the edge of the river, our pastor leapt in and ran across. Mind you, the current was moving swifter than normal, and the water came up to the pastor's chest. The little kids who followed bobbed up and down like buoys while the pastor encouraged them to "just kick a little harder." Somehow drenching my only remaining pair of clothes (or being swept downstream) didn't appeal to me or most of the others.

The trip ended a couple days later, and one of the counselors even got a snakebite as a souvenir. I don't remember the sermons or what any of the meetings were like. It was a trip gone awry, but I have hilarious memories, and friends who made it alive. I have had some of the best times of my life camping, which is why The Rock's summer and winter camps were such a blessing to me.

"Experience the Divine in '99"

Pastor Steve often repeated a statistic that if a teenager attended three consecutive youth camps, there was a good chance they would never renounce their faith. He believed it and as a result we were bombarded by advertisements for winter and summer camps. These camps lasted a week. One was held at a ski resort, while the other was at Covenant Pines Christian camp, both about three hours north of the Twin Cities.

The camps were marketed as spiritual retreats, promising a renewed sense of God's presence. Each camp had its own theme, and they *always* rhymed with the year. We sold everything from wreaths to steaks to kidneys trying to come up with funds for camp. Occasionally one of the generous youth would help another out with leftover funds. The rabid attempts to raise money were all worth it when you handed in your registration and that big check signifying that you had a place on the bus.

Winter Camp

Winter camp was held in February, attracting kids from all over Minnesota. It was a chance to meet other Charismatic youth groups and exchange ideas.

Since Living Word is a nondenominational church, it was interesting to see the differences between affiliated churches and how they interacted with each other. All were respectful and pretty much on the same page, except for one incident involving the Minnesota Vikings losing the playoffs, and seeing how there was a group from Wisconsin, well, it got ugly. . . .

Once again I boarded that bus headed for camp. But this time it was 9 a.m. and I was well slept and ready for a whole four days of goofing off with my zany drama friends. As the trip progressed, joy unspeakable began to build in our little hearts. McDonalds was on the horizon. McDonald's isn't usually classified among the world's finest places to dine, unless you're a 5-year-old with a Happy Meal addiction. But there was something new about feasting at this fast food giant as we arrived. We were going to bombard McDonald's with 100 kids.

I raced with my friends across the asphalt just to see the look on the faces of those dear sweet grease merchants as orders for hundreds of burgers and fries rang through the air. It was well worth it. Voices from the back grill alerted "Here they come!" and "I hate it when they do this!" We looked like the line for Space Mountain at Disney World. People certainly earned their minimum wage that day.

The energy gained from our burger joint invasion reinvigorated us, and allowed us to withstand another hour in the bus. The noise quieted some as most of us were glued to our windows, scanning the scenery to be the first one to spot Quadna Ski Resort.

Quadna isn't a very good name. It doesn't strike any inspirational chords that would make one feel spiritual or even empowered to attempt skiing, but it was a fine place to stay nonetheless. It was a log cabin style facility, boasting nice grounds, an indoor pool, spacious rooms, and a conference center.

We all met in the mess hall for supper and announcements. Pastor Steve stood up and welcomed us, casting a vision in our minds about the spiritual blessing we were sure to get from our guest speaker and the movement of the Holy Ghost. I grinned, knowing what "movement of the Holy Ghost" would mean for our meetings, and just as Pastor Steve was getting impassioned with his welcome a cry broke out:

"There's some guy running outside with no pants on!"

Wouldn't you know it? Some member of the youth group stripped down to nothing but his boxers and went for an evening constitutional as everyone stared out the window laughing, cheering, and totally forgetting Pastor Steve's nice spiritual welcome. I smiled. Things were looking up.

Winter Camp Services

Meetings at camp were always Holy Ghost meetings. Most of the kids who signed up were already full-blown charismatics who craved spiritual expression 24/7. A few visitors came, and usually ended up charismatics by the end of the trip, because they couldn't hide from the moving of the "spirit."

It wasn't 15 minutes before the wailing, laughing, shouting, screaming, and quaking started. As soon as I stood to raise my hands in worship I took a look about the room. To be honest, I couldn't wait for the "spirit" to take

118

over. It was a spectator sport to me, and anticipation for what would happen welled up in my chest and throat until I almost shouted for joy.

The craziest stuff always occurred at camp, and would have kids talking for weeks afterward. That first night was relatively normal, as we enjoyed some praise and worship, people responded, and we heard a good message. But things soon deviated from a normal Holy Ghost meeting.

Service had ended, and it was only about 9:45. How can you go to bed before 10:00 on a spiritual retreat the first night when nobody's tired? The staff thought so too. After a small pow-wow in the back corner of the room, the staff decided to do something special for all the teens too pumped to go to bed. It was decided to have a Christian dance party.

We had CDs from Christian techno groups (yes they do exist), and we turned them on full blast. Soon that boring little conference room was filled with teens on their feet dancing with all their might like King David. One hundred kids swayed back and forth, jumping up and down to the driving beats of cutting edge contemporary music, while some nut flipped the light switch on and off for effect. Of course, an emphasis was placed on dancing for the Lord and not with each other.

We were all pooped when the last song finished. Bedtime was a welcome suggestion. We trudged up the stairs, and stumbled to our rooms to find our precious sleep. There was little talking in my room as everyone slowly undressed and crawled into bed with a feeling of satisfaction for having come. My thoughts drifted to the possibilities for the next day, and I smiled as I closed my eyes.

Another Compromise

The next day brought a breakfast of bacon and eggs. The bacon taunted me as I stared. I had grown up with the health message in my family and in my church. But they weren't here, and I had been a charismatic for almost a year. I was hungry, and I stared at that bacon. Of all the places to be caught holding up the line, it had to be here. My Adventist beliefs had occasionally slipped out and sparked strange looks from people. I hated those looks and wanted to make a full commitment to something. I know it's silly, over something as insignificant as bacon, but it symbolized what was happening to me spiritually. I grabbed two pieces of swine and took my seat among my friends.

It reminded me of John eating the scroll in Revelation. It tasted good, but it felt bitter inside. It was a compromise. I choked it down and occupied myself with conversation and the day's ski trip. I didn't like the feeling I had, but I was a charismatic now, so my heart would just have to deal with it. Besides, after the evening meeting, I would forget all about it.

The Meetings Get Intense

Our drama leader opened the service with a skit about a person being in heaven's file room, witnessing all her sins being recorded. She frantically tore through the files trying to hide her endless supply of sin. Then Jesus entered the scene. The girl burst into tears as Jesus began reviewing. She screamed at Him to stop. To her horror He looks through every single one, even the private sins. Then he proceeds to sign His name in blood on every one.

People were moved to tears and silence. The guest speaker walked up to the podium and told everyone that he didn't need to preach; we just needed to spend some time in worship. High Praize took the stage and played soft worship music while everyone spent time singing, praying, and worshiping.

I have never experienced anything like it. As the meeting progressed you could feel a tangible, peaceful presence rising in the room. I went to my knees, then I laid down flat. I spoke a few words in prayer, but mostly just laid there meditating and enjoying the presence of God. Thoughts of my relationship with Tiffany and my goals in life drifted in and out of my mind. She was still clinging onto me, and it was hard for me to move on. An hour went by. The music kept playing and the atmosphere of prayer intensified. I felt like I was in a spiritual incubator being hatched.

I'm sure the roughness of the carpet made an impression on my cheek as I lay on the floor, but time didn't seem to matter. I closed my eyes and let God search my heart.

As my mind whirled around in the music and the other prayers going up, I decided to sever my relationship with Tiffany and pursue God wholeheartedly. It felt like my conversion experience was being streamlined. Jesus was eliminating everything that held me back from pursuing His will for my life.

The meeting lasted more than two hours. The quiet, thoughtful spirit continued as people left for their rooms. No one spoke, except in whispers, as the music kept playing long after I went to bed. The conference room felt like the Holy of Holies, where the presence of God dwelt. It was a room dedicated to prayer and worship, engaging all our senses and intellect.

Why Can't I?

The final meeting before going home broke out into a session of "praying over" each other. The pastor's wife felt impressed after the sermon to lay hands on all the youth and "speak over them" concerning things in their life, assisted by our prayer ministry leader, a woman in her fifties. We all lined up as the band played, and down the line went the prayer ministry leader and the guest speaker's wife.

Being prayed over was a fairly common occurrence, including ministry practice sessions, altar calls, and of course camps and conferences. A person with the "anointing" laid hands on your forehead, your chest, or your neck and "prophesied" about your life and calling. It stirs an incredible excitement inside you when you believe the person praying is really hearing from God, for whatever that person says will point you in the right direction.

In the Charismatic church, prayer is a very personal thing. When someone lays hands on you they will not only pray to God but begin to "prophesy" things about you. This is quite a deal when you only wanted prayer for a cold and the person praying starts saying that you are called to save the nations and to have millions of dollars for the Lord. It certainly makes you forget about your stuffy nose. You'll hear such terms as "We are going to spend some time praying over each other," or "God wants to speak some things into your life."

I do believe that a person can hear from God and speak things over people that are true. But much of what I witnessed appeared a distant cousin to fortune telling. People lined up at conferences just to have a special person add a mystical quality to their life, pronouncing what God was going to do with them. I was still seeking a lot of answers and was all too eager to get my fortune . . . I mean future . . . uh, my "word" from God.

As hands were laid upon me, I felt no spark or rush, though I tried my best. The prayer ministry leader touched my forehead and started speaking in tongues. Prophecy followed in English. She told me I had a "healer's anointing," and that she saw the elderly leaving nursing homes healed, feeling as young as ever.

I felt ecstatic and wanted to go try out my new anointing. I asked pastors and the guest speaker's wife if I could lay hands on people. They gave an indifferent and less than enthusiastic response. I never got the chance.

Conclusion

Jesus said the truth will set you free. A small seed of truth now shimmered and took root in my heart. If this church believed that they could impart spiritual power to their parishioners, why did they not let me use it? Why did they claim the power for themselves and refuse to empower me? Didn't God want to use my gift? I thought about it long and hard as I went to sleep that night, and chose to forget about it the next morning.

Despite the disappointment regarding my "healer's anointing," Winter camp ended well, and I had lots of pictures and stories to share with my family.

Pride and Seek

Tiffany called as soon as I got back, with a new set of problems for me to sort through. I refused. "Tiffany," I said, "your life isn't my responsibility anymore." Peace flooded my heart as I said goodbye. I knew I had made the right call.

My Ears Itch

2 Timothy 4:3 says, *"For the time will come when they will not endure sound doctrine; but after their own lusts shall they heap to themselves teachers, having itching ears."* A lot of people will tell you anything you want to hear, but they are not friends or prophets. Certainly there are positive messages from friends and teachers, but it is always important to test everything you are told by the Word of God as well as if it comes true.

Many people depend more on their pastors and stronger brothers and sisters in the Lord than on Jesus. They want people to tell them what to do, how to do it, when to do it, and where. I saw many go up to get prayed for and get a different message every time, and none of it was true unless it was incredibly generic. The Bible says to "speak the truth in love." Sure, it might sting a little when someone applies the truth to your spiritual wounds, but the Bible says, "Faithful are the wounds of a friend." In other words, don't just surround yourself with church services, friends, pastors, or teachers who do nothing but butter you up. The ones that are hard to find are the ones that will speak the truth into your life and help you overcome your shortcomings. Seek them out and gain some understanding. Let them kick your butt a little; it builds character.

Chapter 11

Speaking in Tongues for Dummies

"And there appeared unto them cloven tongues like as of fire, and it sat upon each of them" (Acts 2:3).

Shundai (pronounced *shun-die* or *shunda*) is a word you've probably never heard of. It's a word you will probably never feel the need to use. It isn't in the dictionary, because no one knows the definition—or if it's a real word—but it's a word that brought my friend, Brian, and I hours of laughter and joy at Holy Ghost meetings. It's a word we coined, even though it had been used before us, and we spoke it any chance we got. It was a word only discovered when you are in the midst of a church that speaks in tongues.

It is hard to describe tongues because it's not commonly spoken language, and it's not offered in high school as a foreign language credit. I likened it to Spanish because, at least of those I heard speak it, the inflections and cadence are similar. All I knew was that it made my skin crawl when immersed in it.

Pride and Seek

Though Adventists believe there is a need for baptism in the Holy Spirit, charismatics believe that the evidence of the Holy Ghost baptism is speaking in tongues. Speaking in tongues is considered a heavenly language, which contains the "mysteries of God" that the Holy Ghost will interpret for you. In all fairness, many times I witnessed people speak in tongues and then speak things that were quite sound and changed someone's life. Other times . . . not so much.

My pastors and teachers told me never to try and figure out the meaning of the language of tongues, for it was a "prayer language" only the Holy Ghost understood. The phrases used were mysterious, the language of angels! If I tried to dissect it too much I would be in trouble.

My teacher in discipleship class, another youth, made the specific point that unless someone had the gift of prophecy, or could interpret the act of speaking in tongues as a whole message, we shouldn't try to break it apart.

"That means that you don't say 'Shundai' means 'the,' for example," she said. That was the first time I heard the word, and I really didn't think much of it. I might have heard that term in passing once or twice in long sessions of speaking in tongues, but I paid it no mind . . . until I heard a charismatic preacher on the radio. She was preaching away, and after rapping off an eloquent and fiery phrase, she concluded by shouting "Shundai!" People whooped and hollered, and some laughed. I thought it was funny, so I began using it as a slang term among friends.

History of Shundai

As far as I could discern, "Shundai" was a word a charismatic had gotten hold of a few decades ago when the Pentecostal movement was gaining momentum. Most people considered it somewhat flaky, used by exhibitionists. However, if I listened closely to people speaking in tongues, they would often begin their babbling by using that word as an opening. I once saw a light-hearted skit about how to fake being a spirit-filled Christian, rapping off a phrase of real English words at a fast pace, making it sound more or less like tongues. One of the phrases repeated was "I drive my shiny Honda." "Shiny" and "Honda" spoken quickly together mimicked the "shundai" sound.

It didn't take long for this word to spread to my circle of friends, and we referred to Holy Ghost meetings as "shundai" meetings. When we prayed over each other we'd jokingly touch each other, say "shundai!" and fall on the floor twitching. It even became a veggie swear word: "What in the shundai are you doing?"

Some people thought we had lost our minds, until Jesse Duplantis, a major charismatic evangelist, came to speak.

"Do you remember what people used to do back a few years ago?" Duplantis asked, as Brian and I watched from the front row seats we'd managed to snag. "They'd try to figure out what words meant. They had that one word, oh what was it? Shin . . . no . . . shundai . . . oh, shundai!"

Brian and I almost choked laughing. An authoritative source had acknowledged our word.

Pride and Seek

The Usual Practice Drill

I first experienced tongues in the prayer sessions in High Praize practice. Sessions of prayer revolved around every practice, in every church service, and in every ministry. It didn't matter if you were in High Praize, Streetlight Drama, or were the person who made french fries in the café—you were going to pray before you touched anything. And you were going to pray until your ministry leader felt impressed that it was time to stop. It was here that tongues babbled its way into my vocabulary.

Whatever the situation, the drill was the same. Everyone entered a small room off from the lobby and shut the door. After a few minutes of visiting the leader would share a special burden on their heart that they wanted us all to pray for. Then we would all stand, join hands, and the leader would ask one of us to start.

This probably sounds normal to most of you reading this. We've all had "circle prayer" where we go right on down the line until we arrive back at the leader. We even have "popcorn prayers" where everyone just says a short prayer at random, and we arrive back at the leader, who closes things off re-capping what was said. All this happens in about 10 minutes, in a nice orderly fashion, and once prayer is over we finally get down to business. In a charismatic church, prayer is the business.

Actually, let me rephrase that last sentence in the previous paragraph. In the charismatic church, prayer is war. It's not a spiritual burp before or after the main course of church service. They believe that the battle for souls isn't won in an evangelistic series, during the sermon, or even in anointed praise and worship. They are won in the spirit far before any external expression of worship is exhibited. What happens in charismatic prayer was unlike anything I had ever experienced before or even heard about.

My First Encounter

I walked into the small, dimly lit prayer room anticipating an evening of high energy jam sessions. I figured we would spend a few moments in prayer like most Christian groups, and maybe even a little sharing time so I could get to know everybody in the band. I didn't expect to have an encounter with "Spanish" again, but the brothers and sisters there wanted nothing less than a full-bodied spiritual experience.

"Simon, would you start us off?" the worship leader asked a well-built singer. Simon smiled and nodded, but instead of simply saying a few inspirational phrases, he launched into an unknown language. I felt a warm, intruding shudder. I couldn't dismiss it this time. This wasn't Spanish—this was tongues. And it didn't stop with Simeon.

Everybody started all at once, rattling off words, sentences, phrases; continual sounds in a bizarre beehive of babble. I felt like I was in the middle of a spell casting session. The buzzing of everyone murmuring whatever sound came to their tongue created an eerie atmosphere for me. I was so freaked out I couldn't even pray in English. I just wanted to stare. I was frightened, but also curious to observe it, not knowing what might happen.

Pride and Seek

I was expecting a typical "circle prayer" when I was suddenly cut off by people jumping in. I stared at everyone for a minute before joining. I wasn't really sure how to get in on the prayer. Everyone's face was filled with passionate concentration on their praises and their tongue talking. I closed my eyes, found a happy Jesus thought, and began praising God. Was I accepted? Most certainly. My new friends were warm and loving, and smiled when they heard my less than boisterous worship, which, compared with theirs, was barely audible. Did I feel awkward? You better believe it.

My first reaction to participating in the group dynamic was intimidating because it was, in fact, dynamic. But my tepidness didn't last long. After a few sessions lasting an hour or more, I heard reports of all the great things God had shown my fellow Christians, how He laid burdens on their hearts, and how they felt an awesome peace and empowerment. I decided to drop my spiritual tepidness and leap into the heat of spiritual warfare.

Before long, I was shouting praises, Amening, and rebuking every devil in the tri-state area. If I had a burden on my heart I would yell it over the praises. My friends followed with a chorus of "Yes Lord! MM-Hmm Amen!" They stood in agreement with my requests and I with theirs. It pumped me up. I liked being able to speak from my heart in prayer and have others affirm what I was feeling.

Claiming souls was another aspect of our "spirit-filled" prayers. While you would think it was exciting enough to be in a room with 15 people simultaneously praying, yelling, and speaking the Word over anything that came to mind, it gets even better when you add a little soul-winning spice into the mix.

Soul Claiming

A picture of the city of Minneapolis hung on the wall during our Streetlight Drama prayer session. Suddenly one of my friends was overcome with a heaviness for souls. I had never seen tears in a prayer group before. Well, that's not quite true. What I mean to say is, I had never seen sobbing in prayer. I'm not talking about a little "boo-hoo" either. I'm talking about unrestrained, uninhibited bawling. In a matter of 30 seconds we had a reenactment of the Flood. Streams flowed from the wet eyes of the saints in the room praying with me, and all I could think was, *Wow*.

My friends knelt on the floor, laid on the floor, embraced each other, and stood with hands raised to high heaven, pleading mercy for sinners. I don't know how long I stood watching the scene before I realized I was supposed to be praying. I gathered together the few praise-filled sentences in my repertoire, 'cause I was not ready for such a flamboyant display of emotion.

War

I was so stunned at the wailing and passion involved I merely wanted to sit down and observe. Many would label this blatant emotionalism, and wag their head at such a demonstration. I know I would have . . . at first. But then I wondered—if Adventists spent more time in prayer agonizing over the lost, would our churches be as full as those that do? You just can't do church as

131

usual when you walk out of a prayer session like that. You can't just go back to happy-go-lucky cheap talk in the lobby. You just can't not care any more about what happens during the service. About the only thing you can do is go to war.

Watching the Talking

For weeks I observed tongues and the responses it triggered. I saw friends raise their hands and open their mouths to make obscure noises. New converts did it with a look of uncertainty. Speakers said that if you didn't speak in tongues, you were missing something. You were missing the Holy Spirit.

The charismatic concept of tongues is taken from various scriptures and was linked to having a powerful prayer life. They called it your "prayer language," based on 1 Corinthians 14:15, or "praying in the Spirit," based on Ephesians 6:18. They believed the prayer language was God's Holy Spirit praying through you when you didn't know what to pray. By praying in tongues you "edified" yourself (1 Corinthians 14:4) and allowed God's Spirit to pray through you for those things you needed. God would grant you the blessings your life was lacking. You prayed God's mysteries and would bring those mysteries to "manifest" in your life. I was also told that the devil feared praying tongues because he couldn't understand it, for as the language of heaven it had additional powers that the devil or his minions could not handle. I was a Christian and it scared me!

Tongue-speaking was never forced or turned into a salvation issue, but they considered people who didn't speak in tongues as not "spirit-filled," and somehow inferior in faith. They believed that speaking in tongues was the evidence of the Holy Spirit, based on the encounter at Pentecost when the Holy Spirit fell and the disciples spoke in tongues.

Leaders asked new converts and visitors, "Are you born again and filled with the Holy Ghost with the evidence of speaking in other tongues?" This confused most nominal Christians. Naturally the answer leaned towards "No," which provided an opportunity for the leaders at the Rock to share various texts from Acts and Corinthians.

Before I ever spoke in tongues I had the chance to watch others get "baptized in the Holy Ghost" and do it. I was in the backroom (per Tiffany's request) with some other new kids who needed orientation. One of the boys looked like a quivering lab rat waiting for an experiment to begin. He had accepted Jesus in the meeting, and now that he had been whisked away to this room with several others, he looked like he was having second thoughts.

The adult leaders gave a boisterous welcome and handed out some material. Then each Care Pastor knelt down in front of the seated teens, one on one. They had an important question to ask.

"Would you like to be baptized in the Holy Ghost with the evidence of speaking in new tongues?" The teen stared, blank as a piece of fresh notebook paper. Though ads teach teens how to respond to peer pressure about drugs, alcohol, cigarettes, and even sex, few teens learn how to respond if someone asks about tongue-speaking. The leader would get out his Bible and show some verses.

Pride and Seek

In the Hot Seat

You've just handed your life over to Jesus, and you trust the people running the youth group not to tell you anything false. When they pose a spiritual truth to you that seems as vital as your newfound salvation, it seems right to accept it. It also looks as if the Bible itself is telling you that it is necessary, and even if you are spiritually illiterate, the Bible seems the best choice to get information on Jesus. When you don't know much about the Bible it's not hard to be convinced of anything when someone offers a proof text, even if it is out of context.

At the same time, you desire to belong. Everyone struggles to find a niche in life. A lot of kids who came to The Rock had screwed-up families, and were considered rejects at their schools. They suffered from depression, addiction, and low self-worth. They needed love and acceptance. By accepting Jesus Christ they not only fit into God's family now, but this particular church had a special language they spoke from God. How cool is that? A new family, a new identity, and even a new language everybody speaks that only God can understand.

Repeat After Me

Once the teen agreed that they wanted to have this new ability, the Care Pastor asked them to repeat a prayer. Eyes closed, the teen repeated a prayer like this:

"Dear Jesus, I have read in Your word that You want me to be filled with the Holy Ghost with the evidence of speaking in other tongues. I ask you to baptize me, fill me, and anoint me with Your Holy Spirit. In Jesus' name, Amen." Now, after looking at the Bible texts, you'd think a person would just speak in tongues as naturally as burping after a cold root beer, wouldn't you? It should just burst out, right?

After the prayer the Care Pastor launched into his prayer language right in front of the kid who had just asked for a blessing. Kids felt confused as to why they felt nothing happen. I expected to see some great display of power, with some spirit overtaking this kid's soul and forcing him to belt out long utterances in an unknown tongue. Instead we both stared clueless as to what was supposed to happen. The Care Pastor took over.

"Just repeat after me," the adult said, taking over the situation. He spoke loud enough for all to hear. He even annunciated! "Come on, just let it out, just speak in; let it flow!" Apparently the Holy Ghost needed to be coaxed into activity.

The teen gave a feeble attempt, saying some sort of gibberish in a mumble. The adults applauded, slapped him on the back, and said, "You've got it! Who's next?"

I somehow managed to avoid this process of "baptism," but I watched teen after teen say the prayer and make awkward attempts to mimic what he heard the Care Pastor saying. In every case, even the remotest attempt warranted praise and affirmation. A kid could have sneezed, and it would have been credited as the Holy Spirit.

My Turn to Talk

I attended the Rock for five months before I worked up the courage to try tongues myself. By now I had heard nearly everyone speak it, and my feelings of uneasiness and awkwardness had dissipated. I was accustomed to it, like being immersed in another country that speaks another language. I had begun to mumble some of the sounds I heard at times, and in my prayer time I tried to concentrate deeply, hoping that maybe the Spirit would take me over and give me utterance. I finally just decided to mimic what I heard.

I wanted to experience tongues, and I had heard a message that the Holy Ghost wasn't going to "hijack your body" and make you do anything. So I decided to participate, standing there in the back row on the bleachers. I opened my mouth and spoke in tongues.

How Sweet the Sound

It was choppy and strange at first. I wasn't uncomfortable, just uncertain of what sounds to make next. I just had to let my mouth take over. You wouldn't think babbling would be hard to do, but when it comes right down to it you would be surprised how hard it is to come up with nonsensical noises fluidly for several minutes.

Eventually tongues became natural. The more time I spent speaking it and attending prayer sessions and practices, the more new sounds I picked up. I say sounds because it was fast enough to where you couldn't pick out indi-vidual words or phrases. The new language felt good to speak, especially because it made me feel like a charismatic. I was blending in perfectly.

Services took on a new level of fun because instead of staring at people during Holy Ghost services, I could jabber with them and get into the spirit of things, even if I knew I was only mimicking.

In the main church the pastor frequently asked the entire congregation to "pray in the spirit," and everyone would start praying in tongues, 4,000 people all gibbering their hearts out. I gibbered with the best of them, and a sense of belonging permeated every babbled phrase. It was like laughing at a joke you don't understand.

People have asked if I ever felt a spiritual high or a sense of something supernatural taking over my body. To be perfectly honest, and to the disappointment of my Pentecostal brothers and sisters, the answer is no. I never had the sense of being taken over or having my tongue think for itself. I admit that in the beginning, simply because of its newness and the message that it was an angelic language praying out the mysteries of God, tongue-speaking did give me a spiritual buzz, one like you'd get from a really good worship service, but I felt nothing miraculous.

In one service, while I sat next to Brian, the youth pastor told everyone to "Just turn to your neighbor and start speaking in tongues." Brian and I laughed at the bizarre sight of the others rapping off crazy sounds and trying to act deeply spiritual. This didn't make the leadership happy. "If you can't speak in the spirit around each other," they asked, "than how are you going to do it in the world?" It was a guilt trip to keep our developing minds from the absurdity of what we were doing and bring us back to the belief that we were indeed speaking the tongues of angels, and our spiritual lives wouldn't be worth a hill of beans if we didn't. I thought it was strange that we could self-induce the miraculous at anytime.

My Opinion

In retrospect, the tongues I spoke at the charismatic church were not a supernatural display of God's power. It's a learned pattern of behavior. Now I know there are countless studies and books on glossolalia (the scholarly term for tongues), stating all sorts of history and possible explanations for it. But I only claim to be an expert on my own experience, not tongues, being slain in the spirit, or anything else. From what I saw, felt, and had demonstrated I saw tongues as something that was made out to be a divine miracle but was really taught through human babbling and mimicking. The scene of watching kids in that back prayer room being asked to "repeat after me" and having it advertised as "baptism in the Holy Spirit" was outrageous. I never read about Paul giving healing or tongues classes.

I am sure somewhere in history a person had a spirit overtake them. I heard stories in sermons about how the Spirit had jumped on people or moved in meetings and caused all sorts of strange things to happen, including healings as a result of the preacher's handkerchief, raining gold dust, and of course tongues. But in my case, I just wanted to fit in. I tried with all my might to believe it at first; but I never really bought into it. The funny part is, as I "rose through the ranks" in the youth group, taking leadership positions, praying over people, and being slain in the spirit, nobody could tell that, besides my conversion, my experience wasn't real. That's significant for a church which prides itself on its ministers having an "anointing" which grants insights into peoples' lives.

This was not an intentional deception. Up until I was reconvicted on the Adventist message, I did my best to believe the charismatics' doctrine. Even if I didn't feel anything or thought what was going was senseless, I wanted so much to experience what the others around me seemed to be experiencing. I felt like I was the only one who was analyzing tongues when it was being spoken. I just seemed to be missing something. I was held in place from relinquishing my mind over to whatever it was the others were experiencing, and it wasn't just in the area of tongues either.

Talk Like an Angel

"Though I speak with the tongues of men and of angels, and have not charity, I am become as a sounding brass, or a tinkling symbol" (1 Corinthians 13:1). Somehow this text got overlooked when ministers were busy preaching about tongues and labeling other ministries as not being spirit-filled or worse.

A few months ago I tuned into a charismatic radio program talking about living a "spirit-filled" lifestyle. I hadn't been listening for more than five minutes when they started mocking other churches. Instead of referring to Bill Hybels' successful church Willow Creek, the caller and the radio personality referred to it as "Up-a-creek." They went through several other names as well, and it disgusted me, because a church which derives one of its fundamental doctrines out of 1 Corinthians 13 should remember that the very first verse says that if there is no love, the sound is nothing but worthless noise.

I remember sitting in prayer sessions as leaders excused friends and family's less than desirable behavior as a direct result of not being spirit-filled, and I suppose that is correct in some ways. What bothered me was when they began criticizing a local church's failure because they didn't speak in tongues. It's not that there are no churches that fail because they're not spirit-filled (in the biblical sense). It is just when Christians act like their feet don't stink compared to others that makes me mad as a hornet. And Adventists are far from immune.

Have you ever heard someone say, "Well, *they're* not Adventist," referring to some inadequacy in another group of Christians? Half the time if we checked up on our own spiritual sickness, we might be surprised that we aren't the Adventists we thought we were. Spiritual pride is spiritual death, regardless of outward successes. Make sure that when you make a comment in regards to a brother, sister, or church's performance it is meant as help from a friend, not as a smokescreen for your own spiritual athlete's foot.

Chapter 12

Passing Out for Jesus

"The guards were so afraid of him that they shook and became like dead men" (Matthew 28:4, NIV).

A swarm of questions collided in my mind as I lay on the floor. The most important one was, "What do I do now?"

I had gone forward for prayer after service and had someone lay hands on me. I had seen people fall backward onto the floor and expected to feel whatever they felt when they were touched. A "catcher" stood by at the ready.

The pastor was going down a whole string of people lined up in front of the stage, each one passing out and falling backward as he prayed over them. My turn was coming up. Around came the minister's hands, touching people on the forehead as he shouted, "In Jesus' Name!", "Fire!", and "Holy Ghost!" People would sometimes twitch on the way down in the catcher's arms or simply go limp. I wasn't sure what I would feel as my turn came up. Would I pass out? Would I feel dizzy? Would I burst into fits of joy?

Pride and Seek

Hands were gently, but firmly laid on my forehead for just a split second. I braced to feel a burning sensation, or maybe an electric shock, perhaps both at the same time! Instead I felt the mister give a jolt with his arms and felt a slight push on my forehead. "Fire!"

I was startled to be sure, but as far as blacking out or going faint? Nope. So, with a tad more fervency (because the spirit just needed a little encouragement) I was prayed over again, and with a little more purposeful push on the forehead. I took this as my cue to "fall out," figuring that the magic happened on the way down. I did a trust fall into the arms of the catcher, who lowered me to the floor.

I acted asleep for a few moments before cracking an eye open to have a look around. People lying next to me were enjoying the same spiritual blessing I was . . . I guess. They were breathing but motionless. I was at a loss as to what I should be doing, saying, or experiencing. The pastor had started speaking again, people were sitting in their bleachers paying attention, and a smorgasbord of people were still "slain in the spirit" with me. I could only think of one thing to do.

I nonchalantly shifted positions so I could be closer to another fallen out brother and asked, "Can we get up now?"

Why Pass Out?

So what is all this passing out stuff? If you've ever watched Benny Hinn or the Trinity Broadcasting Network, you have probably seen people putting their hands on each other and passing out on the floor. One classic example of this is a clip of Benny Hinn acting like a baseball pitcher, holding an invisible ball, throwing his anointing at an audience member. The person acted like they got hit and passed out. It's a strange phenomenon, and it's a wonder they found any way to construe it out of the Bible. But they have.

When Saul was converted he had an experience with God that knocked him off his horse to the ground. When the followers of God encountered angels they always fell face down in fear until the angel picked them up. At Jesus' tomb in Matthew 28:4, the soldiers fell "as dead men." They weren't dead, but they were out cold. I was told this was where the reasoning and the term for being slain in the Spirit originated. When you encounter the presence of God it is so powerful that you can't help but buckle under the weight of God's glory. Yet one question remains. The Bible doesn't record people who collapsed under God's presence as getting a blessing. People were struck deaf, dumb, and dead. But in a charismatic church people could receive anything from a healing, a financial miracle, to the joy of the Lord by getting slain in the spirit. It all depended on what you wanted prayer for.

It's All in the Hands

The act of "laying hands" is central to being slain in the spirit. In the charismatic church anyone with authority—which includes lay leadership, teachers, and especially pastors—are considered to have the "anointing." They are considered to have great gifts, including prophecy, and because of that, many large name ministers in Charismatic circles are considered and treated as prophets, with just as much authority as someone in the Bible. When they touch you it's as if you are getting a touch from God, and because the touch of God is so immensely powerful, people collapse as if they were dead.

Charismatics are adamant hand layers. I preached at an interdenominational youth rally in Canada, and I saw a few people from an Assemblies of God church talking. One of the ladies had her baby in the stroller and mentioned that it had a cold. The pastor leapt into spiritual action and laid hands on it, rebuking the "demon of sickness" off of it. The baby didn't pass out, but that's not to say the pastor didn't try. He was aggressive in his speech, and if someone decided to interrupt the meeting later on that evening, I knew who could scare them away. Laying on hands, believing that you are administering a holy blow so powerful it not only knocks the devil out, but the believer as well, is an awesome feeling.

Takin' People Out

I had the experience of slaying people in the spirit during a sermon I preached at The Rock. I led an altar call and prayed for people through the laying on of hands. Truth be told, I was looking forward to this part. I was going to bless the socks off people by laying them out cold on the church floor.

A sense of power stirs your emotions when you know you can simply touch people and make them pass out, and in the process heal their wounds, give them wisdom, and set them free. The preacher wields God's power, and his or her touch slashes into the body and soul of those being touched. It's a privilege we all vied for.

As I made my altar call about 20 people lined up in front of the stage, awaiting a touch from God. With the lights turned low and soft worship music playing, I went down the line touching people. Some stayed standing, but one girl went limp and collapsed into the arms of a catcher. All I could think was, *Wow, I have the power.*

I continued down the line, getting more fervent as I went. I shouted things like "Holy Spirit!" while grabbing someone gently on the sides of the face. I hollered "Healed!" as I touched someone's forehead. I even laid hands on one girl who had no catcher behind her. She fell over, just barely catching herself before she would have smacked the back of her head on the floor. Thankfully she was unslayed long enough to brace herself, before she laid back down and went to sleep. At the end I wished there were more people to slay.

Power, Power, Power

Power is intoxicating. I saw ministers line people up so they could race down the line pushing them over. They loved the power, and it wasn't until I did it myself that I understood. I also understood why they never let me pray over anyone at camp. If I did, it would take away their power, and if I had the power, then I got the attention. I saw other kids ask for opportunities to pray over others, opportunities to prove their anointing, opportunities to affirm their closeness to God. Most of them were denied.

My Opinion

But the question remains, for those people who did pass out or go into fits of hysteria, what actually happened? For me it is a similar answer to the speaking in tongues conclusion, with the addition of some powerful suggestion. Sermons and services focused on emotions. People were taught that the power of God has a weighty effect. Pastors even told the congregation to let God "stir up your holy emotions."

They saw people fall out when hands were laid on them, and to top it all off the senior pastor, the pastoral staff, and every guest speaker promised and marketed themselves as having the "anointing." When you sit in the middle of all that, it casts in the depths of your mind a belief that God works supernaturally through Christians' hands. A pastor once told me that the only things you needed for a healing ministry were faith, a hand, and a sick person, and if you don't receive anything from God, then somehow you missed the Spirit and it's your fault. When you get called forward for prayer in front of 5,000 believing people, you wouldn't want to look unspiritual by not reacting to the laying on of hands, or make God's messenger look bad.

The power of suggestion is very strong. One day I had an interesting conversation in the car with several other leaders in the youth group. As we sat in the parking lot they expressed doubts over being slain in the spirit.

"When I get prayed for, and I don't fall down, I can feel them start to push. I don't like that," a friend remarked. I was stunned. I thought it was only me, because I knew how Adventists believed, and had not grown up in the Pentecostal church.

"Why is it some pass out and some don't?" someone else asked. "If it were really God's presence, wouldn't we all pass out?"

"Yeah, and I don't pass out like some do," yet another continued. "I just lay there uncertain of what I should be feeling. And when I do get up, nothing is ever different. I'm not sure what is supposed to happen, but they just tell me my faith isn't strong enough, or that I started doubting and lost my blessing."

That was enough for me to begin making conclusions. Being slain in the spirit was a mixture of suggestion, false doctrine, and emotionalism, wrapped up into a neat little package of heresy, that hurting, needy people were all too willing to believe.

As my time at The Rock continued the slain in the spirit concept faded rather quickly. I felt at home speaking in tongues, but I rarely went up to get prayed for, despite enjoying praying for others and wielding the mysterious power of heaven with my hands. About the only thing I did get out of the slain in the spirit doctrine was a chance to catch up on my sheep counting.

I once decided to self induce a slain in the spirit experience while my teammates prayed in the spirit. I had arrived at practice extremely tired due to a grueling week at school and was in no mood to participate in a rigorous prayer war. So, when everyone began to pray, I got in the spirit.

First I sat down, making sure that I had a deep, passionate expression on my face. Then I went to my knees for a few minutes, just as everyone else was working themselves up into a frenzy of prophesying, crying, and speaking things over the ministry. Finally I arrived on the carpet with my face to the side. I laid there for about 25 minutes catching a marvelous nap, as all the while people thought I was being ministered to by the Holy Ghost. I must confess, I got the idea from a youth pastor who used that tactic when the head pastor's wife expected him to have something to say after prayer sessions. He would simply fall out, and pretend to be in the spirit while someone else got stuck sharing. It works.

Falling on Your Face

John 4:24 says to worship God in "spirit and in truth." Believe it or not, there is a lesson in all this falling down stuff. The word for worship used in the New Testament is *proscuneo,* which means to "prostrate" oneself before God. The act of worship does involve a bit of being "slain in the spirit," but not in the passing out sense. To me a real "slain in the spirit" experience is when God becomes so awesome in your soul that you humble yourself by laying your pride flat on its face. Don't be afraid to have the occasional kneeling or bowing down session to remind yourself that God is above all things.

Chapter 13

Drinking for the Lord

Drinking makes such fools of people, and people are such fools to begin with that it's compounding a felony (Robert Benchley).

When I was 9 years old, I was struck with an incapacitating case of the giggles. It happened during my mother's piano practice. I was sitting there minding my own business when suddenly it came to me that leaning backward on the piano bench would be an excellent idea. I gracefully hooked my legs over the surface of the bench and hung by my knees with the top of my head touching the carpet. My mother gave me an odd look. The look filled me with glee, and I started to laugh.

Soon I was laughing so hard I couldn't stop. The mixture of my mother's look, boredom, and the blood rushing to my head gave me a fit of giggles. Even when my mother got up and left to do something else I remained hanging upside down, gasping between giggles, trying to regain composure. To make matters worse I couldn't get up. I tried to sit up, only to be tickled again and swing back upside-down. It was a solid 15 minutes before the glee subsided enough for me to topple off the bench and onto the floor. I felt dazed and drunk after the experience, and enjoyed it so much I looked forward to it happening again. The charismatic church was glad to oblige.

If You're Happy and You Know It

Teens still lingered in the Rockatorium after the sermon. Pastor Steve invited anyone who desired prayer to come forward, and he would touch their forehead with anointing oil. That sounded neat, so with my curiosity leading the way, I knelt down and got my blessing.

Once again, though I tried my best, I didn't feel anything special, but everyone else around me started acting funny, laughing and doubled over. Some even rolled on the stage. Not knowing what was going on (and not liking it one bit), I started laughing; not real hard, but enough to fit in for about two seconds. Yet instead of the laughter subsiding after a couple moments, it intensified. People flopped over each other, unable to stand up. Things were getting creepy, and I started checking the vents for noxious fumes.

I lay on the stage, pretending to laugh along with them. A girl's leg landed on me and stayed there for several moments—the six inch rule wasn't enforced if the Holy Spirit was prompting the touch. I must have been there for nearly a half hour before people either passed out or staggered out of the sanctuary like they were drunk. Which brings me to the granddaddy of bizarre false doctrines: being drunk in the Holy Ghost.

The Toronto Blessing

Remember the evangelist who yelled "Fire" at everyone, and they all passed out? The guy who helped the lady in the balcony realize her blessing was on the floor? Pastor Rodney Browne helped instigate the Toronto Blessing.

Pastor Browne was known for inspiring listeners to go buck wild, and one of the pastors of a large church in the Toronto area visited Tulsa, Oklahoma (a hub for charismatics), and fell under Browne's influence. Soon Pastor Browne came to preach in Toronto where, following a message, people broke out in dancing, hysterics, roaring, and even barking. This was considered a "move of the spirit." It was dubbed a blessing and made headlines in the Pentecostal arena. Soon other churches were vying for this experience.

And who wouldn't? I mean, wouldn't it be interesting to see the Dorcas ladies dancing on the altar? How about your head elder barking at the head deaconess? Wouldn't it be amazing if the people in the balcony roared, while those down front passed out with delight?

The Ramifications

I admit it would be nice to preach a sermon to my congregation that would warrant such a response. There would be no question you hit a home run on the pulpit if Sister Ethel did a cartwheel down the center aisle during the closing hymn. There's only one problem. As far as I can tell, it's just another twisting of scripture revolving around the Pentecost account.

Acts 2:1-13 tells of the outpouring of the Holy Spirit on the disciples on the day of Pentecost, which caused them to speak in various languages they'd never understood before for the benefit of foreign visitors. Verse 13 says that some people mocked them, saying that the disciples were drunk. Ephesians 5:18 says that we are not to be drunk, but rather filled with the Holy Ghost. Pentecostals believe that this means there's a parallel between being drunk in the flesh and being drunk in the spirit. One charismatic minister even reasons that "If there is a way to get drunk in the natural, there must be a way to get drunk in the spiritual." There are even websites with prayers asking for it. One website's prayer reads, "Make my cup overflow and make me drunk in the Holy Ghost." Basically this means that you can act out of you mind without limits (save hurting people).

Taking a cue from Nehemiah 8:10, *"The joy of the Lord is your strength,"* charismatics consider it a blessing and an empowerment when someone erupts in laughter due to an anointing of joy.

Don't Mind if I Do

About the drunkest I ever got was at winter camp, during an outbreak of the Holy Spirit. I had been watching others act drunk and it made me laugh. People then thought I was drunk, so I went along with it. It wasn't hard to keep the laughter up when everyone else was acting nutty, and surprisingly enough, when you really want to act drunk, it isn't all that hard.

Brian and I crawled up the stairs, laughing and laying hands on each other (because that is what you do if you want to keep the "anointing" flowing).

We got to our room, helping each other stand up as we swaggered around being imbeciles. After awhile I needed a drink of water and sauntered out in the hall. I was alone, with no one around to egg me on and no one to pay me attention.

I really felt no drunk feeling anywhere in any part of my body, except perhaps my silly mood. But I wanted to fit in. I wanted to have the same experience and feel what they felt. I wanted to be drunk, and I had a mind to act it out even if it wasn't so. I laughed, crawled, and swayed down the hallway to the water dispenser and got a drink, repeating my antics all the way back to the room. Wanting to fit in can make you abandon reason.

After awhile I laid off the holy booze and became a spectator. Oh sure, I would run up and touch people, yelling "Fire!" just to see what they would do, but I rarely handed myself over to be subjected to "new wine" and the shenanigans that went with it. They would have to catch me off guard, and then I would go along with it just to get them to leave me alone.

The Process

Once, after Wednesday evening "healing school" in the main sanctuary, I got caught. I had walked over from The Rock to meet some friends and decide if we were going to Applebees. I encountered two adult leaders from The Rock, drunk and laughing themselves into a stupor with my friends. *Uh-oh,* I thought to myself. *Here we go.*

Sure enough, they spotted me and came closer. One was crawling on all fours. The other two were hunched over. If this scene had occurred on a street with people I didn't know, I would have run away or grabbed a stick and prepared to defend myself. With their arms outstretched, my friends looked like grinning zombies.

They immediately laid hands on me and forced me to go through the process of getting drunk. My friends breathed out heavily, like they were warming up for a workout or getting ready to give birth. I went along with it so I could get it over with and go to supper.

After the breathing it is good to hunch over a bit. This slow crumpling of one's posture tells the person laying hands on you that the spirit is moving and is having an affect on your state of being. The leaders started laughing, almost as a call to get me to laugh, so I laughed too. I figured that once I had a good laugh for a few moments I could get undrunk and go drive.

Acting drunk in church is a strange feeling. The meeting rooms looked like a battlefield after a conflict. Bodies lay everywhere, some still, some twitching. People laughed and cried. It's scary at first, but after awhile you learn to simply step over everybody and dismiss it all, for "the Lord works in mysterious ways." At least that's what they told us when we questioned why God would inspire such disorder.

What Would Jesus Drink?

"Whatsoever ye do, do all to the glory of God" (1 Corinthians 10:31).

Does the president send an ambassador to another country drunk? Would

Jesus want His ambassadors to a dying world passing out, laughing maniacally, and staggering around drunk when they are supposed to be representing Him?

I believe there is a clear distinction between drunkenness and being filled with the spirit. The Bible consistently calls us to be sober, ever watching for our Lord Jesus' return. I want to make sure that nothing I do hinders or distracts from the Gospel I am called to preach. May we all, by God's grace, represent our King positively in thoughts, words, worship, and action.

As my senior year of high school approached, I began to wonder if this church really reflected how Jesus would act.

Chapter 14

Spiritual Harassment

"My soul had been stirred within me by what I heard. And so deep was the sense of conviction in my heart, that I feared the Lord would not spare me to reach home" (Ellen White, commenting on a sermon about the Second Coming, *Testimonies,* vol. 1, p. 15).

"He who will not accept advice and counsel from God's human agents is in danger of not receiving the counsel of heaven, and will be fatally mistaken unless his spirit is changed. He will look upon others with suspicion, thinking they are in the wrong. . . . Christians should be teachable, they should have self-control, they should ponder upon that which is presented to them, and fear that their own course may not be perfect, when they see so many defects in their brethren that leads them to accuse and condemn" (Ellen White, *Testimonies to Southern Africa,* pp. 46, 47).

My senior year passed swiftly. I counted down the milliseconds until graduation, when I would be released from the pubic school system and into a private Christian college. I was sick of the secular and wanted to spend all my time in an atmosphere of faith, instead of just a few weekday evenings. It's not that there is nothing good in public school, but as I pursued God's will for my life, I began to see the benefit of studying where I could form my faith with teachers who cared for my spiritual life.

The Search for School

Schools started calling me. Each day I would come home, snatch my mail from the table, lay on my bed, and begin looking through bulletins, programs, and letters for a glimmer of my future.

For a long time I believed it was God's will for me to find a job that made the most money possible. The charismatic church emphasized excellence and striving to be the best, and I figured there was no better indicator of job satisfaction than your tax bracket. I considered business. I had talked with owners of Mercedes dealerships about their operations, and spent quality time on my school's career search program, scanning everything from entrepreneurship to administration, all the way down to llama breeding.

By April I'd decided that I was born to go into marketing. I had read that a good marketing executive could make a nice chunk of change, and if that wasn't the Lord's will, than what was? Now I just had to narrow down the schools to find the best possible program. I wanted a Christian college, and I wanted to stay local. After all, I had my social life planned out for the next four years, and having to make friends all over again would be about as much fun as a poke in the eye. It seemed easy enough, but as I perused Christian colleges' materials I flipped past other programs that gripped my attention—namely, pastoral ministry.

"Let's see," I mused to myself as I flipped through one school bulletin. "Biology, business, nursing, Biblical studies . . ." I spent five minutes reading through all the Bible classes offered before I snapped out of my trance. "No, no, I need business majors." I flipped back to the beginning of the bulletin and started over.

"Administration, accounting, small business management, marketing, pastoral studies . . ." I had drifted off again. For some reason I always seemed to find the theology and ministerial programs fascinating. Greek seemed more interesting than math, and preaching more appealing than business law. But I refused to let myself get carried away in these areas.

"No, I want to make money. I will help *fund* churches, not run them."

The Call

This routine went on for several weeks until one day, after staring at a pastoral care major for 30 minutes, God impressed my heart with a question: "Are you in this for me, or the money?" Suddenly that feeling you get when you've just lied to get away with something stirred in the pit of my stomach. I knew the truth. I knew where my heart was, and I knew where God wanted me.

Fine, I thought. *Looks like I'm going to be a pastor.*

Confirmation

"We have been praying for you to figure that out for months!" Pastor

Steve exclaimed when I shared my decision. It was an affirmation I needed, and I began to feel a great peace. But I wasn't thoroughly convinced. I had been onstage several times during drama performances, but I needed to try preaching. To me it would be the ultimate test of my calling, so I expressed interest in a Teenpastor meeting and was scheduled to speak.

Looking back, I'm amazed to think of how much I changed from the middle of my sophomore year. I went from being uncomfortable, unnoticed, and uninterested in what God had to offer, to the person leading worship for 300 people. Who knew that God could change a person so much? But as I began preparing my first sermon with the enthusiasm of a puppy with a T-bone steak, the Holy Spirit started asking questions. As I began studying the Bible for my first sermon, the Holy Spirit began troubling me about truths I had abandoned and tried to forget.

Sunday vs. Sabbath

When I came to The Rock I was a prideful, hostile Adventist, but now I was a regular Sunday worshiper. I attended Sunday morning service faithfully, and the Sabbath I grew up with was taking a rest of its own. Growing up I had never watched television, shopped, or did anything secular on the Lord's Day. Now I spent Saturdays doing whatever I wanted, never thinking of doing anything special to honor the One who had not only created the Sabbath but re-created my heart.

Now I slept in while the Adventists I grew up with reached out and gave to others. Saturday became all about me, instead of all about God. Sunday was God's day now. I went to church twice that day, fellowshipped with friends that day, and nearly forgot all about the seventh day of the week. I was planning on keeping my knowledge of the Sabbath a secret for when the Mark of the Beast came, and then I would start going to a Sabbath-keeping church—you know, once the tribulation began.

Diet vs. Pig Out

I used to think that eating pork was the cause of sin in the world. After a year of pepperoni pizza I thought that perhaps pigs were just a misunderstood source of nourishment. It smelled fine, looked fine, and tasted fine. While I never ordered it myself out of a lingering conviction, when anyone asked if I'd like pepperoni on my pizza, the reply was always the same: "That'll be fine."

I gave the same answer for ham, bacon, sausage, crab, or anything else that was once alive but now found its carcass on my plate. Ever since the bacon incident at camp, I was open to any meal suggestion, as long as it wasn't raw. For once I felt normal. Growing up my family was forced to badger waiters, hosts, neighbors, and anyone else cooking to see if the hot dogs were "all beef." Now I could simply walk up to the grill and pick out anything I wanted. It didn't matter anymore, except when I got a queasy feeling in my chest that I knew didn't come from the food.

Peculiar vs. Bizarre

It is peculiar when you are the only one in your school who goes to church on Saturday. It is peculiar when you are the only kid on the playground who has no recollection of or anticipation for Saturday morning cartoons. It is peculiar when everybody says how glad they are that their grandparents are up in heaven looking down on them, when I know for a fact that they're underground waiting for Christ's return. It is peculiar growing up Adventist, and I was glad for a change. I was glad to be bizarre.

It's bizarre when people shudder or look at you in awe when you say you speak in tongues. It's bizarre to pray for your friends and instead of thanking you, they pass out at your feet. It's bizarre when the adults in your church don't sit still, but run around and laugh like 5-year-olds. Being bizarre did warrant bizarre looks from time to time from people I got to visit my new church and participate in the worship experience. But I was happy, wasn't I? I just had one little problem: I couldn't shake my stupid conscience.

As I worked on my sermon and worked on keeping the truth in my heart from surfacing, I began to really struggle. It was like packing away bundles of clothing into a suitcase for a vacation, then not being able to close it. No matter how many times you sit on it, smash it down, or jump on it, the dumb thing pops open so you can't leave. My heart knew the truth, and although I had stifled convictions, smashed down my beliefs, or jumped up and down on what I had been taught, it kept popping out. I wanted to go on a vacation from the truth, but some force wouldn't let me pack.

Pride and Seek

I had ignored it right up until spring of senior year. Whether it was a Holy Ghost meeting, being slain in the spirit, or laughing until my eyeballs exploded, I went along with everything. When someone talked about the secret rapture, I kept my opinions a secret. When someone referred to Sunday as the Sabbath, my skin crawled, but my face stayed cool and my voice silent. When my friends talked about people being in hell or dying and going to heaven, I wanted to share the truth with them so badly, but all I could muster was a nod validating their beliefs. I loved my friends, my church, and my new life. I loved them more than I loved God.

So once again, just as He had convicted me of my need for conversion, just as He had called me to pastoral ministry, God brought one more big life changing conviction.

The Return of Adventism

At Adventist campmeeting that year a pastor announced that he would be planting a church in the area. It would be more contemporary in style, with contemporary worship music, and a radical stylistic departure from traditional Adventism. This concept appealed to a number of people, including my family.

No one in my family had attended church regularly for about six years, so when my dad mentioned his interest in this new church I was taken aback. I had never known an Adventist church to resemble anything that would strike me as dynamic or relevant. I had been struggling with letting go of my Adventist beliefs and couldn't manage, but as far as the worship style and spirit of the charismatic church went, I was right at home. Now Adventists were changing the way they did church? Were they becoming what I was used to?

I felt a strange longing in my heart. Somewhere deep down I wanted to be in a church whose beliefs were tested by scripture, not by whatever vision or interpretation popped into the pastor's head by his "prophetic anointing."

Aside from inner struggles with doctrinal issues, I hadn't thought about Adventism for four years. All of a sudden my family was getting involved and sharing with me all the wonderful plans being made . . . without me.

I was surprised at how much it bothered me. I belonged to the largest, most explosive church in the state, and a church that didn't even exist yet was pulling on my curiosities. I tried to ignore it. But the church planter got in contact with me, wanting to hear about the youth ministry I was involved in. The Adventist message was bubbling and stewing in my heart, wanting to burn away all the "new truths" I had accepted—truths that were about as biblically sound as the assertion "Moses was a woman."

The Church Plant

One lazy Saturday afternoon I agreed to go with my family to this church planting pastor's house just to see what it was like, and offer any input toward developing a youth ministry. I was ready to wow them with my expertise from the big league church.

I expected to tour some stellar facility, with a professional band playing the hand-clapping, foot-stomping worship music I was used to. I pictured the pastor wearing an Armani suit, living in a quarter million dollar home, beckoning us into his own personal conference room to discuss the dreams we had for this groundbreaking new church.

Nope. He was middle-aged, slightly balding, owned a keyboard, lived in an upper middle class home, and drank soy milk. The conference room doubled as the living room, and he wore shorts and a t-shirt.

Grumbling to myself as I entered the home, I shook hands and forced a smile, acting overly spiritual. The home was nice enough, but not gaudy or humongous. As I sat on the couch I noticed I was the only one under 35, or dressed professional enough to discuss starting an organization, and I grumbled again. These people didn't want my input. They were old.

Dashing My Expectations

After 15 minutes of small talk I learned the pastor was a vegetarian and heard a sampling of the music that was to be "contemporary." I had expected to hear southern black gospel style music with powerful voices and emotional vocal fills, or praise music that would leave people raising their hands for more. Or perhaps a melodic worship song, accented by strings, and a worship leader with an 8-octave range and a 30-piece ensemble. What I got was canned music.

I tried to act excited about their plans, but the whole operation felt beneath me. I was used to catered conferences, live music with a full band, and stage lighting, with more than 4,000 people in attendance. Moreover, I was used to what every successful ministry needs to be spiritual: a huge budget. Standing in that home studio I got the same embarrassing feeling I used to get when my parents tossed out surfer slang like "awesome" and "tubular" in front of my friends and me. It reverberated with every note of prerecorded music. I didn't realize it, but my spiritual pride had come back, and was blocking my ability to see this group's potential for influencing my life in a way I never thought possible.

Just when I was about to give up, I was given the opportunity to talk about my experience at The Rock. They listened. The pastor asked me questions. Some adults grew bored as I talked, yet others made comments and took mental notes. By the end they had asked me to help start a youth ministry at the church. For someone thinking of pursuing ministry, an offer to be a youth pastor and occasionally preach was golden. I accepted, and I couldn't wait to inform my friends at church that I had moved beyond drama and Teenpastors and was now truly in the ministry. Maybe I would be able to help change these Adventists for the better as well—after all, as a "spirit-filled" Christian, I had the market cornered on spirituality.

The Rock's Response

My leaders and friends at The Rock responded with more concern than adulation. They had severe reservations about the Adventist church and gave me several warnings to be careful. Although they tried to act happy for me, some people expressed deep irritation. But for the most part, my friends overlooked it, and supported me.

Pride and Seek

I now understand why they were all concerned. The Bible says you cannot serve two masters. Meshing my charismatic experience with Adventism only magnified my inner struggle. I taught the Sabbath one day, and the very next attended Sunday church. I taught the state of the dead, only to support friends who said their loved ones were in heaven. I taught on the Second Coming at the church plant, and claimed to be "rapture ready" at The Rock.

My first two sermons were scheduled within a month of each other, one at The Rock and the other at the church plant. I was attending four services per week, in two different environments. My spiritual growth came to a halt and turned into more of a spiritual inventory. I found it harder and harder to ignore that I didn't believe everything the charismatic church taught. The Adventist pastor began suggesting I consider Union College. I promptly shot the idea down. My friends at The Rock were going to attend Oral Roberts University, and were motioning for me to do the same. I needed to do something drastic to get Adventism off my back.

Making the Call, Getting Called

I applied to Oral Roberts University, much to the disappointment of the Adventist pastor—and much to the delight of my friends at The Rock. I would go to Tulsa, Oklahoma, and pursue ministry there. I had decided wholeheartedly after preaching my first sermons that pastoring was my calling, and I wanted to get far away from the SDA atmosphere that kept creeping back into my life. I had my finances worked out and was all set. Except for the reoccurring phone calls.

Union College had begun calling me late in the spring, and even though I had told them I was going to ORU, they seemed rabid about getting me to come. The chair of the religion department even called me. Who were these people? Was I being stalked? All I wanted to do was shine my charismatic light in front of the nice little Adventist Church plant—I didn't want to get recruited back to the faith! Yet just as God had worked through Tiffany to get me back to church, God was now using the church plant to bring me back to the three angels message, and Union College was blowing the trumpet.

Some colleges make it difficult to communicate your displeasure with them. *I did not want to go to Union College!* Sure, the church plant was fun, but it ministered more to people in their 40s and 50s, not to me. I was happy for them and their innovative ways to reach older Adventists, but they had nothing for me. I was trying to help them—right?

One day a Union College recruiter showed up at my door. What was he doing here? I thought I told these people "No!" The recruiter told me about all the opportunities ministerial students enjoyed at Union, how great the spirit was, and how much I would enjoy it. I had to resist with my strongest defense yet. *Seth, it's in Nebraska. What would you do there? Forget about it.* Yep, those were words of wisdom, tried and true.

What would I do in Nebraska? What would I do in Adventism? Attend churches dressed in the best the 1970s had to offer? Snore my way through my own lifeless sermons because they had been choked out by rigid exegesis? Dust off the old hymns and groan out their dead notes for a half hour? Attend church on the Lord's Day . . . eat food I know the Bible says is OK . . . hear the truth grounded in scripture for once . . . and maybe end my spiritual harassment? No! I didn't want to be an Adventist! I had to get away.

Thankfully summer camp was coming up, and I could immerse myself in nothing but the best my church had to offer—and lose sight of what my heart was telling me. I could have fun in dynamic worship services, get a spiritual high, see miracles, and maybe even get the chance to pray over someone. Yeah, summer camp would be the answer.

Too bad you can't run from God when He has determined to catch you.

Flesh Fight

"Watch ye and pray, lest ye enter into temptation. The spirit truly is ready, but the flesh is weak" (Mark 14:38).

The charismatic church made frequent reference to "the flesh," and the battle between the spirit of God and our natural tendencies to sin. It's a difficult struggle—especially when our flesh wants something that appears to be positive. A large scholarship awaited me at a great college. I really wanted to go, but in my spirit I knew it wasn't right. In my spirit I knew that it was a good school and I would be blessed if I attended, but it wasn't what God wanted. I've walked away from relationships, jobs, opportunities, and experiences that laid themselves at my feet, yet weren't what God wanted. And as a follower, everything we do is about what He wants.

The flesh doesn't always try to trip you up with the stereotypical drugs, alcohol, and sexual promiscuity. Sometimes it simply presents selfish options in light of what God is calling you to do, and you must resolve to follow God's leading. What God wants is always better in the end.

Chapter 15

Summer Camp Escape

Summer camp was almost identical to winter camp, except with a location better suited for outdoor activity and a bigger emphasis on evangelism and commitment.

At 9:00 a.m. we boarded that familiar bus with the green vinyl seats and musty smell, ready for a good time. After a word of prayer we took off and lurched onto the highway, prepared for three hours of yelling and wisecracks. Nothing out of the ordinary happened until my friend Wendy fell asleep.

Falling asleep on a bus is seldom safe, no matter who you're with. We took it upon ourselves to wake Wendy up. The trouble was, she was a stubborn sleeper, immune to the typical tickling, shaking, cheek squeezing antics that would wake most people.

I put my headphones on her and cranked the Star Wars anthem to top volume. Nothing. I tried snapping the headphones on her head. Nada. We placed her finger up her nose and took a picture. No response whatsoever. It wasn't until we tugged at her shoes that she finally snapped awake to our uproarious giggling. She only managed to glare at us before she nodded off again. I was having fun and beginning to forget my convictions.

Covenant Pines

Upon arriving in the wooded glen that was Covenant Pines, we were told to wait in the bus. My voice was hoarse from yelling, and everyone else was stir-crazy from having sat so long. We accommodated the request to wait for about 12 and a half minutes before we started rocking the bus and climbing out the windows.

We grabbed our stuff and made our way onto the main campus. It had a large lakeside lodge where we checked in. The boys cabins were lined up next to each other close to the lake. The girls' hotel-like lodging facility was behind the boys' cabins, in a wooded area. The bathrooms and the chapel were off along the lake about 50 yards up from the lodge. The sun shone through the whistling pine trees, and a twinge of mischief was in the air.

After registering, pulling on my camp T-shirt, and slinging my pack over my shoulder, I traipsed along the path with the others to find my cabin. Every year the drama guys were placed together with Fred, the drummer from High Praize, as our counselor of sorts. The environment couldn't have been more exceptional for off-color jokes, pranks, and nutty behavior.

I walked up the concrete step toward the green screen door and opened it on its creaky hinges. Boy, was that air fresh! A whole year had gone by and there had been nobody to clean save the spiders. I stopped for a moment, pondering events such as the Teenpastor retreat at a four star hotel and how nice the winter camp resort had been. Apparently the church meant business when it said summer *camp*.

Cracks spanned the length of the concrete floor. The bunk beds were rustic, and the mattresses lay lifeless and stiff. Cobwebs, remnants of curtain, and dingy windows gave the streaming sunlight a dirty yellow hue, but also added to the ambiance. Now all it needed was the presence of vibrant living beings.

Enter the drama guys.

We all dashed to get the top bunks. Not just for safety reasons, mind you (one year a top bunk collapsed on a bottom one), but also to avoid any confrontations with potential forest critters coming to call. That, and it was easier to trick people on the bottom bunk. I managed to snag one and so did my friends Brian and Jeff. We didn't have any time to get goofy, though, because supper and the welcome meeting came in rapid succession upon arrival.

Eating, as could be expected, was a hullabaloo. Ninety kids scarfing down the camp delicacies could only be described by a phrase my dad has used to describe our family's eating habits, "feeding time at the zoo." Meanwhile my friend Jeff unveiled a new trick, which he performed at every meal. Sneaking up behind people, he'd grab their sandwich, corn on the cob, or hot dog, and take a bite out of it. Then he would laugh hysterically and run away. It was always funny—until it happened to you.

Summer Camp Services

The meetings were much the same as the ones at winter camp, with a warm welcome, announcements, and drama. The Holy Ghost was free to move after the drama team performed yet another hit, creating an atmosphere of laughter and freeing everybody from the lingering stresses of travel.

A street witnessing group planned to go into the nearby town of Aiken, Minnesota, for those who wanted to share their faith. They called it "Tak'n Aiken." Paintball, inflatable sports, and Jet Skis were all available for those who wanted to participate. And they were going to inspect our rooms.

They would enter our cabins during breakfast and make a running video commentary on the state of affairs. The cabin with the worst review and rating got KP duty. This was not a camp that would make you want to explore the darker side of the culinary arts either. They had leftovers as old as the trees. And alive.

The winners would get to go through line first at lunchtime and have a chance to win best cabin, which meant an assortment of prizes. By the way, cleanliness was not necessarily the path to success. The judges freely admitted to taking bribes such as money, candy, and any other gifts laid out for them. They would show the bribes in the video to inspire us on how we could forgo the inspectors' wrath. I am happy to say we never lost, and we gloated like heathens when someone else did.

Evenings in the Drama Cabin

After the meeting ended, we made our way back to the dark cabin. There was no light and the bumping, bonking, and banging around filled the woods with the sounds of "Ouch!" "Agh!" "Argh!" Upon settling into bed the joking and pranking began. We had to suppress our mirth though, for Paul (the big doorman at The Rock) prowled the grounds at night to catch anyone on the lam. One of us would make some wisecrack or pass air to the delight of our bunkmates, when all of a sudden a massive beam of light blazed through our windows, moving back and forth light like a giant light saber. "What's going on in there?" Paul's voice boomed.

We pretended to be asleep and made no response, as this might warrant an invitation for Paul to come in and "hang out" with us. If that happened all joy would end, and we'd hear timeless classics that always started with "When I was your age" or worse, "If I was your age . . ." The horror was unspeakable. Once Paul passed, we resumed our lunacy.

Mornings and Afternoons

As the sun popped up, we sprang from our slumber and lumbered to the mess hall, still in our pajamas. We felt giddy showing off our funky PJ bottoms and seeing our female friends in their pretty pink kosher PJs before dining on scrambled eggs and . . . bacon. Whistles and hollers bounced off the walls, but we gave it up so we could enter the building like civilized people. Some of us with a surplus of self-esteem left their hair in its natural state, which added to the happy spirit of breakfast in the lodge.

Jeff managed to take a bite out of three pieces of toast before somebody threatened to plant him six feet under. I continued to get to know a girl named Rachel who I was slowly taking a shine to, and was feeling my freedom as I flirted with new faces.

The afternoons were spectacular. Inflatable sports were set up all over campus, with sumo wrestling, jousting (where two people stand on opposing pillars and try to knock each other off with large padded sticks), and a race that involved being harnessed to an inflatable structure with a bungee cord. You competed against another person by racing down an inflatable track and placing a cloth bar on a piece of Velcro, which was on the divider between you and your opponent. The object was to put your piece further up the divider before being snapped back by the bungee. The lines were long, but we just chatted while we waited in the warm sun.

Camp reminded me of the way they did church. There was a structure, but it wasn't so rigid that you couldn't do what you wanted to do. You could participate with all the enthusiasm in the world, or not participate at all. No one would push you.

Pride and Seek

The counselors let us roam. Enough adults walked around to ensure there was really nowhere to get into trouble. There were also meetings or meals every couple hours so we didn't just fritter away our days. It had the feel of Bible Conference or an extended Youth Rally. We weren't saturated with activities, crafts, or sports. There were always options, but no crazed pastors or camp directors ran around yelling, "Where are you supposed to be?" We could be anywhere we wanted as long as we didn't go off into the woods and still attended the worship services.

Worship Services

Advertisements for the camp centered around the guest speaker, the miracles God would work, the decisions for Christ, and the promise of a life-changing experience. The games and camp amenities were always in the background. We all knew God would touch our lives. The latter part of summer camp carried with it an unexpected spiritual blessing.

During a Holy Ghost meeting, the associate youth pastor spoke something over my brother and I. He said we needed to reconcile and that we had some things we needed to get straight. He felt impressed that we should hug and pray for each other. Normally I would have felt awkward doing such a thing, but the pastor was right. They hit the nail on the head for once! Maybe they did have the gift of prophecy!

Growing up, my brother and I fought constantly and put each other down. I was particularly mean and spiteful, and looked for any chance to get into a fistfight. I needed to seek forgiveness from my brother and let him know in some way that I cared about him and was glad he was attending the camp. I hugged him and although it was weird, it was right, and he forgave me. Later that week my brother decided to get baptized and commit himself to Christ. I was proud of him. I began to feel at ease with my decision to attend ORU and remain in the charismatic church, until my heart was broken at the last meeting of camp.

Spiritual Healing?

Everyone had been praying in the meeting, until someone had the unction to walk over to a boy in a wheelchair. People laid hands on him and began to pray for his healing. Soon others followed, adding their own hands.

The prayers grew into shouts. "Walk in Jesus' name! Walk!"

Soon the same pastor who had prayed over my brother and I, was at the wheelchair's side praying fervently for a healing. It didn't take long before the whole place was shouting and yelling for God to heal this boy. His face turned red as he prayed harder than anyone. Not knowing what to do, I marched over and prayed as well. I prayed believing. After 15 minutes they lifted the boy out of the chair.

The pastor acted as a brace and marched that kid up and down the sanctuary. He moved a little as people screamed for joy. Apparently a twitch of the foot qualified as a healing. I stared. *The boy can't support himself, can't walk, and yet God has worked a miracle?* They placed the boy back in his wheelchair, "healed," and stated, "There are some natural processes working themselves out right now, but he has been healed!"

They nicknamed the boy "New Legs." Unfortunately his new legs had spokes and rubber wheels attached. I thought God created natural laws and could bypass them, right? Isn't that what makes something a miracle? I guess they thought Father God wasn't as big as Mother Nature. I didn't know what to do. This was worse than my "healer's anointing."

I watched the boy get ready to leave camp the next day, still confined to his wheelchair. How could I promote this? My trust in the beliefs and practices of this church faded. How could I stay here? How could I operate as a minister promoting these types of "healings"? I couldn't, but one element that I knew deep down I would have to choose against still held me in place.

God and God Alone

Despite my disappointment, camp always had the highest anticipation of any event The Rock did. People understood that God was going to be experienced, not just talked about. God was going to be exalted, not the programming. People attended because God would be there. The God-focus left issues—issues like behavior, responsibility, appropriateness, standards, and participation—undiscussed. They were just understood.

Chapter 16

Friends Are Sticky

Of all the things which wisdom provides to make life entirely happy, much the greatest is the possession of friendship (Epicurus).

"The warmth of true friendship . . . is a foretaste of the joys of heaven" (Ellen White, *My Life Today*, p. 204).

Statistics say that a person needs at least 7 close friends at church if they are to stay and become active members. Seven friends to attend with. Seven friends to participate with. Seven who do things outside the church walls. Seven to share life with. Sadly, even many pastors don't have seven friends in their congregation.

The Rock had the best facility, the most dynamic worship services, and the neatest programs for people my age, but it wasn't until I made those heart connections with my brothers and sisters in church that my involvement, my attendance, and Jesus Christ became the most anticipated joy in my life.

It's easy to leave a church. By today's standards of entertainment, the church cannot compete. No matter how dynamic the service, the movie theater will always win out in terms of sheer entertainment. By today's standard of having everything our way, right away, from fast food to custom-built financing plans, the church doesn't stand a chance, because sermons, if done well, will make us uncomfortable and call us to change and do things God's way. The only thing the church has the market cornered on is love. 1 John 4:8 tells us that God is love. If God is the source of love, His church should be a place to come in contact with it through His people. The world's lusts can't compete with God's love. I found that out when I met my friends in my new church, and when I tried to leave.

The Meeting Place

Whether it was drama, Teenpastors, or simply attending church service, I had a Heinz variety of friends. In my three years at The Rock I developed significant friendships. Nothing bonds you to people like working for God together, sharing the same victories, challenges, and—of course—food.

I'm not sure who started the tradition of going to "'Bees" after Sunday night and Wednesday night church, but I am grateful. I solidified more friendships over the supper table than anywhere else. We came in droves and I was surprised on my first time out that the Applebees staff knew us. They always anticipated our arrival, due to the obscene size of our party and that we all came from the same church. Occasionally other patrons grumbled, "It's the holy rollers."

After church, 15 or more of us would work out the details of who would drive who home so they could go out to eat. Upon deciding ride situations, we evaluated who could afford to eat out and who couldn't. If someone couldn't pay, someone was always willing to cover the expense. It reminded me of the early disciples, meeting in small gatherings and providing for one another's needs.

I believe there is a power in "doing lunch," because of how simple it is to invite a new person to attend, and how easy it is to talk over a good meal. Conversations ranged from church services to cell phone plans. Occasionally the pastor showed up and greeted us all for awhile before he found his own table. We could get a bit rowdy at times with frequent spills, barnyard noises, and laughter so loud it made your ears bleed.

Sticky People

Brian was my best friend. He was just a tad younger than I, but twice as mischievous. Brian and I stalwartly supported each other when it came to women. If I had a crush on a girl, it was instantly ratified by Brian. On the other hand, if one of us labeled a girl as crazy, the other would agree and keep their distance. We laughed our heads off at worship service idiosyncrasies that most people didn't notice, warranting several glares from other worshipers who obviously had no ability to laugh at themselves.

From drinking four bottles of sparkling grape juice in one sitting at New Year's, to breaking up with our girlfriends at the same time at summer camp,

Pride and Seek

Brian and I shared a bond that created an atmosphere of mirth and spontaneity wherever we went. This made for delightful church services and social outings, and made the more reserved members of the Body of Christ cringe.

Isaiah was a combination of joy and weird. He was a normal looking kid most of the time. But when he got a certain look in his eye, he gave performances that would make people in rubber rooms look normal.

While dining at Chili's one evening, Isaiah got the urge to do his fly buzzing up and down the window impression. Chili's was particularly busy that evening. We had 10 at our table alone. As everyone was enjoying intimate conversation at the bar or at their tables, Isaiah went right up to the window with the wooden shutters, folded his hands in front of him, and began to make buzzing noises.

"ZZZT! ZZZZZZZZT! ZZZZZZZZZZZZZZZZZZT!"

Silverware clanked on plates, drinks spilled, and one lady softly said, "Oh, my goodness." Thankfully he stopped before our waitress came out of the kitchen, and we enjoyed the rest of the meal as normal people would.

The identical Phad brothers were as skinny as bean poles, but their hearts were fat with God's love. They were readily available to give rides to church, parties, and anything else one might need. They hosted big get togethers at their house and faithfully show up if you planned one at yours. They were our Switzerland, always neutral when friends squabbled. They gave their advice and stayed out of people's business. If our circle of friends was a company, the Phads were the support staff.

Adam and Tom were the nice guys of the group. We could heap teasing upon them, and they would take it in stride, smiling. We were quick to affirm Tom and Adam, of course, before onslaughts of insult only friends can give each other without fearing offense They were always available to lend you a couple bucks, and would play along with Brian's and my craziness even if they didn't get it.

Bope went by his last name for reasons unbeknownst to us, looked the part of the stereotypical computer nerd, and always brought the most beautiful women to school banquets. There was Nick, Nathan, and of course, Rachel.

The Princess on a Hill

Rachel was the girls' ringleader in my circle of friends. She was tall, smart, and had a smile paralleled only by the sun. She could be wild and crazy, but she also carried herself with confidence and decorum. Rachel lived in a huge house on top of a hill in the country. It had a small farm attached, and was the closest dwelling to a fairy-tale castle I knew of.

I had become a ringleader and spokesman (of sorts) for the guys in our circle of friends, and so, by virtue of our group dynamic, Rachel and I started spending time together developing a purposeful friendship. It started at summer camp (right after Brian and I broke up with our girlfriends), and continued throughout the months of July and August.

Rachel's house became the site of weekly get-togethers, sleepovers, pool parties, and any other excuse to hang out. We were grateful for her parents' philosophy that "God gave us this house to use for Him," because our youth group used it nearly every other day.

One day Rachel invited me to come see one of nature's miracles in progress. I asked what it was, and with a hint of laughter in her voice she asked me, "Have you ever seen a cow give birth? And watching the movie City Slickers doesn't count!"

"Sure," I said, lying through my teeth. "I seen 'em all the time at my grandparents' farm, one right after the other." The answer pleased her, and she invited me to come over and watch. Truth be told, I had never seen my grandparents work on their farm, nor had I witnessed the live birth of a bovine. If it weren't for City Slickers, I would have still thought that cows laid eggs.

I arrived wearing my nicest khakis and button up shirt. *Um, note to self: Farms have dirt. Dirt has a magnetic attraction to khakis. Don't wear khakis on the farm.* Rachel leaned on the wooden fence that held the cows in. She smiled at me, then made a sly comment about the dirt on my pants, almost knowing that I wasn't used to farm life. I brushed it aside and said something like "Bah! It's no big deal!" This was also a lie—one of many that day. The fact of the matter was that I only owned one pair of khakis and wasn't adept at doing laundry. My mother would be angry to have to wash the mess, and I only made enough money at the time to put gas in my car and pay insurance. If I kept it up, I'd have to go without pants.

I leaned over the fence with Rachel and smiled. It was a cool summer day in the country. The clouds drifted lazily by, and Rachel was lovely. Her soft, sweet spirit shone through her eyes and smile. Pretending to watch her father in the pasture, we traded subtle glances, trying to catch the other looking at us without getting caught ourselves. Oh yeah, it was a moment. Just the country farm atop a hill next to the whispering woods, the balmy summer wind, Rachel's hair like brown wisps of silk blowing gently in her face, the nervous feeling of new love swelling in our hearts, . . . and the loudest flatulence I have ever heard ripping through the stratosphere.

Nature's Miracle

Apparently the mother cow had to get rid of some, well, stuff before the miracle came. That heaving heifer was twice normal size and did not resemble the usually happy cows of chocolate milk commercials. This cow had a situation.

Then the man whose daughter I was trying to win walked right over to that cow and put his hands in an area that made me flinch from 50 feet away. Rachel looked at me and said, "The good part is coming up." I willed my eyes to stay open.

The hardest part of all this, including the noises, the placenta, the reaching and the grabbing around, was acting like I was having the time of my life. "This is great!" I said. My stomach told me otherwise. It was like someone rubbing an onion in your eye and then saying you can't cry. It was like eating a block of bitter baking chocolate and being told to maintain a smile while chewing. It must have been love, because no other force on earth would have

Pride and Seek

been strong enough to keep my lunch from going on a reunion tour.

The moment of delivery is almost too horrible for words. Like a squatting weight lifter in the Olympics, Rachel's dad went through a grab, snap motion, and one big slurping noise later, out came a baby calf, covered in mess and gasping for air. I wish I could say it was beautiful.

From organizing group events together, to marathon phone calls, to working together in Teenpastors, Rachel and I were the constant focus of pointed comments from friends intended to expose our romance. We enjoyed simple conversations over dinner with her parents at their hilltop home and laughing while on the swings in her backyard at sunset. Rachel and I grew close, and it didn't take long before we admitted our feelings, but we still paused when it came to a formal relationship.

The Gang That Stuck Like Glue

It would be hard to leave my crew of friends. I had worked three years to amass them all and for the first time in my life I was not only accepted, but loved. I was popular. I was a leader. I could have stayed in high school the rest of my life and been content. For the first time in my life, I felt "in place."

I had brought a negative attitude to The Rock at the start, and their intimidating practices certainly hadn't helped matters. The only person I really knew at the start rejected me. They preached different doctrines than I believed, and they were so much bigger than anything I was used to. I had every reason to get up and walk away. No one would have noticed if I'd slipped through the backdoor Even after I rededicated my life to Christ, I still faced struggles. My friends supported me and held me fast.

Choosing Between God and Man

Aristotle once said, "What is a friend? A single soul dwelling in two bodies." He was right. As my relationships grew at The Rock, my reality became intertwined with my friends. We were all inseparable. They were my home away from home, my adopted family, and nearly my entire support system. The thought of college in general, much less a denominational switch, frightened me.

I had taken solace in the fact that several others from The Rock were going to ORU, and it would only be a year or so until Rachel would attend, and only a year after that when Brian, Isaiah, and the others could come down too. We'd reunite, I'd marry Rachel, graduate as a pastor along with Brian, and along with the others recreate the same little world we had in Minnesota. My plans were perfect, but they weren't God's plans.

Even though our friendships had exploded over the weeks after summer camp, the thought of stepping out of God's will loomed over me. As much as I loved my friends, they could never take the place of God, and the more I thought about it, the more inevitable a decision seemed to be. It's not easy to choose God over loved ones, but as Jesus said in Matthew 19:26, "All things are possible."

Chapter 17

I Give Up

"He must increase, but I must decrease" (John the Baptist talking about Jesus, John 3:30).

I don't like to lose an argument. As a matter of fact, I hate it. I hate it, hate it, hate it, hate it, hate it. The word argument is derived from an old French word, *arguer,* from the Latin *argutari,* meaning to prove or make clear. In modern English it describes a process of reasoning. This means that if you lose an argument, your ability to reason is clearly flawed, and as an individual with a male ego that translates into just one thing: stupid.

If I lose an argument, even over something as trivial as whose turn it is to clean out the cat's litter box, I take it personally, and have been known to respond by one of the following techniques.

The first action when losing an argument is to respond by name-calling. This usually works because it is off the subject, and the other person is so appalled that you would give such a low blow that he stops talking. This lets you get your last two cents in before the next argument-stopping action.

Walk away. That's right, just walk away. Even if the argument isn't heated or the person you're arguing with hasn't finished talking yet. People will generally keep yelling so you can hear them as you put distance between them and yourself. This makes them look crazy, because if someone nearby makes a comment, you can simply deny any knowledge of who the yelling party is. A nice addition to this concept is to walk back to the yelling party with an observing party and ask your arguing partner if everything is ok. In order to do this you must master the last technique.

Find a thought completely unrelated to the topic being discussed, like Christmas, and spend some good quality time thinking about it. Anything works, really, as long as it's a good thought, and you can do it while staring at the other person. It seems like you're paying attention, when you really have visions of sugar plums dancing in your head. (Note to self: Don't let the wife read this paragraph.)

All this expertise in losing arguments doesn't mean I never win. I win a lot, actually. But if I were to list all the people who have bested me in a disagreement tournament, the list would be longer than a lecture on the finer points of gum chewing. Especially if I listed all the times I lost an argument with God, like when He finally convicted me on where I needed to be.

The Phone Call
The swell of unease about pursuing a degree in ministry at a charis-

matic college, followed by a pastorate in a tongue-talking church, had reached a breaking point. I stood in my living room, contemplating my next move, having just hung up from yet another call from Union College. My attempt to escape the conviction through summer camp had backfired, but now all my friendships had been strengthened to the point of having a viable second family. Still, they didn't know I was struggling. As much as they held me in the charismatic church, they couldn't hold the truth back from my conscience.

Would I be happy if I went back to Adventism? Would I be frustrated? How would I make any friends when I didn't know any Adventists my age anymore? How would I work out the finances? What would I tell people? How could I abandon everything I have worked for for the past three years? How could I leave my friends? Will anyone be able to understand me if I go down to Union? Am I just being sentimental for my childhood church? The questions came two by two like animals to an ark, and I didn't have the answers to accommodate them. What I needed was a sign.

"Look, I will put a wool fleece on the threshing floor. If there is dew only on the fleece and all the ground is dry, then I will know that you will save Israel by my hand, as you said" (Judges 6:37, NIV). But what sort of a fleece did I have? It would be ridiculous to set out my Old Navy polar fleece and check it for dew in the morning. I needed something pertaining to college, something pertaining to the situation. I needed another phone call.

No college, no matter how desperate for students, calls again within a week once a student has made it expressly clear that he or she is attending another school. *Lord, if you put Union College on my phone within the next seven days, I will transfer my enrollment from ORU to Union College.* As I got up off my knees my unease was replaced with a new special feeling: paranoia.

Every time the phone rang my mouth went dry and my heart raced. "Uh, who is it?"

"Is the decision maker of the household available?"

"Whew," I said, hanging up the phone before the telemarketer could say another sentence. "Thank goodness it wasn't an important call."

Whenever the phone rang over the next 48 hours I'd answer, mutter a phrase of relief, and hang up on people. I started to feel at ease. This wasn't so bad. I had settled the matter. Satisfied, I sprang into the shower with a smile the next morning and prepared for my day. Yet as I wrapped a towel around myself and proceeded to exit the bathroom to select an outfit suitable for an aspiring Pentecostal minister, the phone rang.

I let it ring a couple times. I felt funny. I didn't want to answer. I looked upward, wondering if this was going to be Providence. I wondered if my arguments, protests, and finely tuned ability to ignore God was about to be shut down. I wondered . . .

"Hello?"

"Hello, may I please speak with Seth Pierce?"

"Speaking . . ." My mouth went dry again. I gripped the phone tight, ready to hang up if necessary.

Pride and Seek

"Hi, this is Union College, and we were just wondering if you were coming down to attend this fall?"

"..."

"Mr. Pierce?"

". . ."

"Hello? Are you coming down?"

"Yep."

Making the Switch

It took about 20 minutes to call ORU and cancel my enrollment, and another 10 to confirm my place at the College of the Golden Cords. It would take much longer to explain my decision to my entourage of friends and leaders at The Rock.

The first person I called was Rachel. Thankfully she trusted me enough to support me in my decision. "If that is what you are called to do, then you need to do it," she said. It was a vote of confidence I desperately needed. I called Brian, and he too backed me up. He even got excited for me as I told him about the peace I now felt in my heart.

For the most part my good friends supported me. A few acquaintances demonstrated disapproval by interrogating me and telling me how the devil works through signs and wonders too, and that my "sign" might be from the forces of darkness. Looking back, such a comment seems ironic from people who believe acting drunk in church is a sign of spiritual power.

The Teenpastor Conference

Holding onto your convictions and values in this world is nearly impossible, especially when onslaughts come from people you respect. I had surrendered my arguments to God, and now He had confirmed in my heart that my decision was what He wanted. I knew I needed to be in the Adventist Church. I had won my peace and direction, and I was determined to go, even against pressure to stay from people I loved.

That year's Teenpastor conference held particular excitement for me, as I was graduating from the program and would be recognized at their huge banquet. I also looked forward to a dinner cruise with my fellow seniors. It's a wonder I didn't get indigestion.

"Would you like some ribs? They're our specialty!" said the smiling chef on the boat.

"Uh, I'll have the chicken." I smiled weakly. Knowing looks from Teenpastor leaders, who believed the Adventist church was a cult, seemed to eat into the back of my head. I sat down quickly with my kosher dinner and said a long blessing to buy time and settle my heart back down.

When I opened my eyes, I noticed that the congenial conversations that usually attached themselves to my friends and I were minimal. More questions were coming, and I had to answer confidently.

"How do you know you're called?"

"I prayed, I meditated, and I feel a peace in my heart."

"But aren't they a cult?"

"Actually, if you know anything about their doctrines you know they are quite biblical."

"But what about ORU?"

"That's not where I am supposed to be."

"But how do you know that?"

For a group of Christians claiming to be "spirit-filled" and having the "anointing," they sure seemed confused about the basic Christian practice known as hearing from God. The questions went around in circles until I changed the subject and went out on the deck of the ship to think. This might be a long weekend.

The following evening, before the banquet, an associate youth pastor pulled me aside, concerned and irritated. "Seth, I heard what you are planning to do, and it's important that you know some things." He quickly opened his Bible to Psalm 1 and read,

"Blessed is the man that walketh not in the counsel of the ungodly, nor standeth in the way of sinners, nor sitteth in the seat of the scornful. . . . Therefore the ungodly shall not stand in the judgment, nor sinners in the congregation of the righteous. For the LORD knoweth the way of the righteous: but the way of the ungodly shall perish."

"Seth, they don't teach the Bible. They teach some things that are contrary to God's Word, and the Bible says that if you sit in their counsel, you won't be able to stand." There is nothing like being told you're going to hell to help cement a conviction from God. I knew he was only sharing what he felt was right, and I knew he cared about me. But I also knew the truth, and I had to respond.

"Actually," I replied, "I've studied their doctrines and found them to be quite biblical." The conversation ended with a deep sigh from me and a walking away from him. *Come on God, I made the right choice, how many hoops do I have to keep jumping through? I can't take much more of this.*

The banquet was a surprise and a much needed pick-me-up. I was greeted by the smiles of my goofball friends, all dressed up to the nines. I had purchased a new suit, shirt, and tie, and received several whistles from women I wanted to receive whistles from. People talked to me, and didn't ask any more questions. My close friends who had always supported me made sure I was close by them, and they gave me enough smiles to last until our faith in Christ unites us in heaven.

My dad showed up at the banquet, along with my brother, who had just entered the program. Their presence meant a lot to me, because they both knew the choices I'd made. My dad had expressed his joy at the decision I'd made. I needed them there, and God provided.

When the awards portion of the ceremony started, a quiet anticipation descended on the room. The awards involved all sorts of Teenpastor categories, from best team to Teenpastor of the year. The "Excellence in Ministry" award spanned the entire youth group. It was given to a youth leader who exemplified excellence in their field of ministry, with one nomination from each ministry. When they announced my nomination for

Pride and Seek

Streetlight Drama I nearly spilt my water on my lap, and when they announced that I had won my mind went blank.

For once in my life I was speechless. Standing up in front of 130 clapping loved ones I would soon leave behind was too much. It was an affirmation I needed. Despite disagreeing with my decision to switch churches, they still had some support for me. I babbled my way through my speech. I might as well have broken into tongues, because I had no idea what to say and what I did say probably didn't make any sense. *They still like me, they still really like me.*

One Last Sermon

Two weeks before I left for college I preached the worst sermon, technically speaking, in my entire career. It was at the church plant and it was my farewell. I don't remember my topic; I just remember being five minutes into it and wishing I could crawl under a pew and hide until the closing song. *Lord, if You are looking for a good time to come back, now would be that time!*

I had told all my charismatic buddies about it, and they all piled into their cars on a Saturday afternoon to come watch. I should never have boasted about skills to people the way I did. I had only done this twice before, and the third time was far away from the charm.

However, after the torture had ended, people came up and told me how my talk spoke to their hearts. How it touched them. How it made them think. A spiritual lesson cemented itself in the sidewalk of my biblical knowledge. God would be with me no matter what I did, as long as I served Him the best I knew how. God will pick up what we miss, He'll clean what we can't scrub, He'll scratch where we can't reach, and He will touch what we can't touch, if we only surrender ourselves to Him.

Moving

Packing for college was traumatic for my mother. I remember seeing a book in her bookcase titled "Letting Go." I nearly had an anxiety attack as well. I had never seen Union College, I didn't know anybody, and I had been away from Adventist culture for so long I didn't know what to expect, but I found it thrilling in a way. Before I walked down to the car where my dad waited to drive me, my mother handed me a letter and prayed with me, sad to let me go, yet joyful at my choice. I was leaving home, yet I was staying. I was going to be an Adventist again, yet applying my experiences in the charismatic church to my ministry.

I took one last look at my apartment and my friends. I still had hopes for romance within my circle, namely Rachel, who stood by to watch my dad and I drive away to an entirely different world. I felt a pang of remorse. I looked my friends up and down and began to realize how much I would miss them. I wanted them to come with me. I hugged each one tightly and then faced Rachel.

I put my class ring in a small satchel, held Rachel's hand, and slipped the ring in her palm. She looked at me puzzled.

"Keep this for me until I get back." I smiled. Then I left my Old World behind in an Oldsmobile, and set out with my father, feeling a bit like Christopher Columbus searching for the New World. I would be back for sure, but when, I didn't know. I also didn't know if I would be different. But I did know that my friends would wait for me at least until I stopped coming back.

Can't Go Back

Somewhere along the line someone told me, "You can never go back home." Life is a living, breathing, changing entity; things never stay the same or as you remembered. This is a truth some churches need to understand and indeed I needed to understand, as Christian culture shock blew me against the walls of my dorm room.

The food was vegetarian and even vegan, a word I had never heard before but, tasting some cheeseless lasagna, I quickly understood as evil. Instead of the latest architecture and technology I'd grown accustomed to, I was greeted at church by, well, the red, er, orange, um reddish orange carpeting I'd grown up with. The praise music was worshipful enough, but no one shouted or even clapped. Sometimes people slogged through hymns like they had just survived a mortal beating.

I wore my ORU sweatshirt to theology classes and got stares, especially from professors. A couple people teased me about it in a good-natured way, but I took offense. *Why do churches give off negative images about other churches?* I wondered. I remembered how most Adventists viewed Pentecostals. It made me want to wretch. While most people saw charismatics as a group of emotional, possibly demon-possessed lunatics, I saw friends. I saw dynamic, growing churches. I saw memories, I saw joy, I saw a bold faith. I wanted to scream at any self-righteous person who thought he understood charismatics and tell them that it wasn't they whom God used to bring me into a saving relationship with Jesus. It was the church that invested three years of time, money, and energy training me to serve God, instead of throwing me into youth Sabbath school in a church basement until I was old enough to be an elder. I wanted to go home.

Despite participating in clubs and a play at Union, my thoughts, letters, and prayers all went home. I could not relinquish myself to the Adventist lifestyle. I just wasn't used to it anymore. Even though there were nice people, helpful professors, and people who respected my background and thought it was cool, it wasn't home. So, after three months at Union, I resolved to visit The Rock on my next break and ask about some local charismatic colleges. I was not going to attend another semester. It was just too hard to let go of the past.

Going home proved more confusing than helpful. I had been writing Rachel regularly and had professed my love, only to hear no more from her. I found out she had been spooked by such a serious comment from a lonely man who was having trouble fitting into his surroundings (due to his lack of effort). I wanted my past to come along with my future, and the stubborn thing wouldn't budge.

I toured a charismatic campus in downtown Minneapolis and wasn't impressed. Back at The Rock leaders greeted me with half-hearted hellos. Some of my friends were gone to college and my acquaintances that remained scrutinized everything I did like I was a science project. The Holy Ghost meeting that night had no affect on me. I couldn't get excited. I didn't believe in what they were doing. I felt lonelier here than I did back at Union. At school people at least tried to be accommodating and inviting. Some of them even said they didn't want me to leave. As I stood in the church hallway I realized that this wasn't home anymore. I didn't have a spiritual home anywhere. I was homeless. It is a scary feeling when you don't know where to go.

Surrendering Again

"God is ready to assume full responsibility for the life wholly yielded to Him" (Andrew Murray).

There are times in everyone's life when you want some direction so bad that it wouldn't matter if someone told you to jump off a cliff. You'd just be so happy knowing what to do that you'd fling yourself off without a second thought. As Christians we sometimes reach a crossroads, and after exhausting ourselves with our own reasoning and processes of elimination, all we can do is cry out, "Thy will be done on earth as it is in heaven," and truly mean it, no matter what the cost.

I prayed hard on the way back to Union to finish the semester. I just wanted to be in God's will. I reflected on when I first came back to church and how good it felt to finally gain direction and purpose in life once I surrendered my life to Jesus. I thought back on how I came to the decision to attend Union as well, how good it felt to give up rationalizing and simply ask God to show the way. On the way back down to finish what I thought would be my last semester at Union, I opened my heart and just asked God to point me in the right direction. I no longer cared where I was, as long as it was with Him.

The Doors Open

Within two weeks of being back at school, I received at least two offers to preach at other Adventist churches. Somewhere along the line the recruiting department at Union got hold of my name and wanted me to do ministry—ministry like I was used to at The Rock. I didn't know they let students preach here, much less pay for them to go out of state. I was going on the road—the right road.

After I started preaching more opportunities presented themselves. The more I participated at Union with an open heart, the faster God opened doors. I started receiving opportunities I never had at The Rock. Friends multiplied like rabbits; good friends, including my future wife. The less I struggled against God, the more blessings fell into my lap. God's will was being confirmed left and right.

I started to feel happy about being back in the church. I started feeling comfortable at my new school. I started feeling at home. I started understanding that God's will can only be achieved by unconditional surrender of the heart, and even if He makes you move to Nebraska, His ways are always the best. Before the semester ended I threw away my ORU sweatshirt and bought a Union College one. I had given up, and God was lifting me up. As soon as I decreased, He took His cue and increased. I began to realize the awesomeness of how God works to save His children in mysterious ways. God had put together a custom built plan just for me, just for me! While monitoring 6 billion people, all the galaxies, and heavenly beings, God designed a plan just for me. He'll do the same for you if you let Him.

I Surrender All . . . the Time

Jesus told his disciples, "I have told you these things, so that in me you may have peace. In this world you will have trouble. But take heart! I have overcome the world" (John 16:33, NIV). Trouble can come in confusion, loss of identity, relationships, spiritual pride, lack of strength, lack of understanding, false doctrines, keeping your convictions, and trying to decide where to go, but take heart—Jesus knows where you are. He never leaves you nor forsakes you.

Since my conversion and rededication to the Adventist message I have had struggles like anyone. Life isn't perfect by any means. I face bills, work, school, writer's block, and two kittens that enjoy jumping around my house knocking things over. But whenever life gets too much for me and I feel confused about where I need to be, I know all I have to do is surrender my heart and open up to God's suggestions. He always provides a way out, always opens a door, always nudges me in the right direction.

I love my Adventist faith and the Adventist family. I love knowing that I am where God wants me to be. And even if I don't love surrendering when I know I have to, the results are always worth it. When I surrendered to go to the charismatic church God blessed me with a new perspective. When I surrendered to commit my life to Jesus, He blessed with a new life. When I surrendered to the call to ministry God blessed me with peace and direction. And when I surrendered to the conviction of the Holy Spirit, I was blessed to be in a church that I know has a special mission from God. Surrender will always be the key to success.

If you are uncertain of where life is headed, what you should be doing, struggling with a decision, or struggling with God Himself, chances are you have passed over the right answer several times, but you don't like it or it scares you. Trust God. He knows what He's doing, and a testimony and a place waits for you in heaven with your name on it, if you are willing to surrender your will, your hands, and your heart. Give up, and let Him lift you up.